Thank you for purchasing this learning book of the basic arab alphabet letters.

we have designed this book specially for beginners to train and write the arab letters without difficulties.

we sincerely hope that this book will be of great use to you.

in order to improve our content, we would be grateful if you could send us your suggestions in amazon comments.

good learning and
see you soon for level 2

Ahmed

THIS BOOK BELONGS TO :

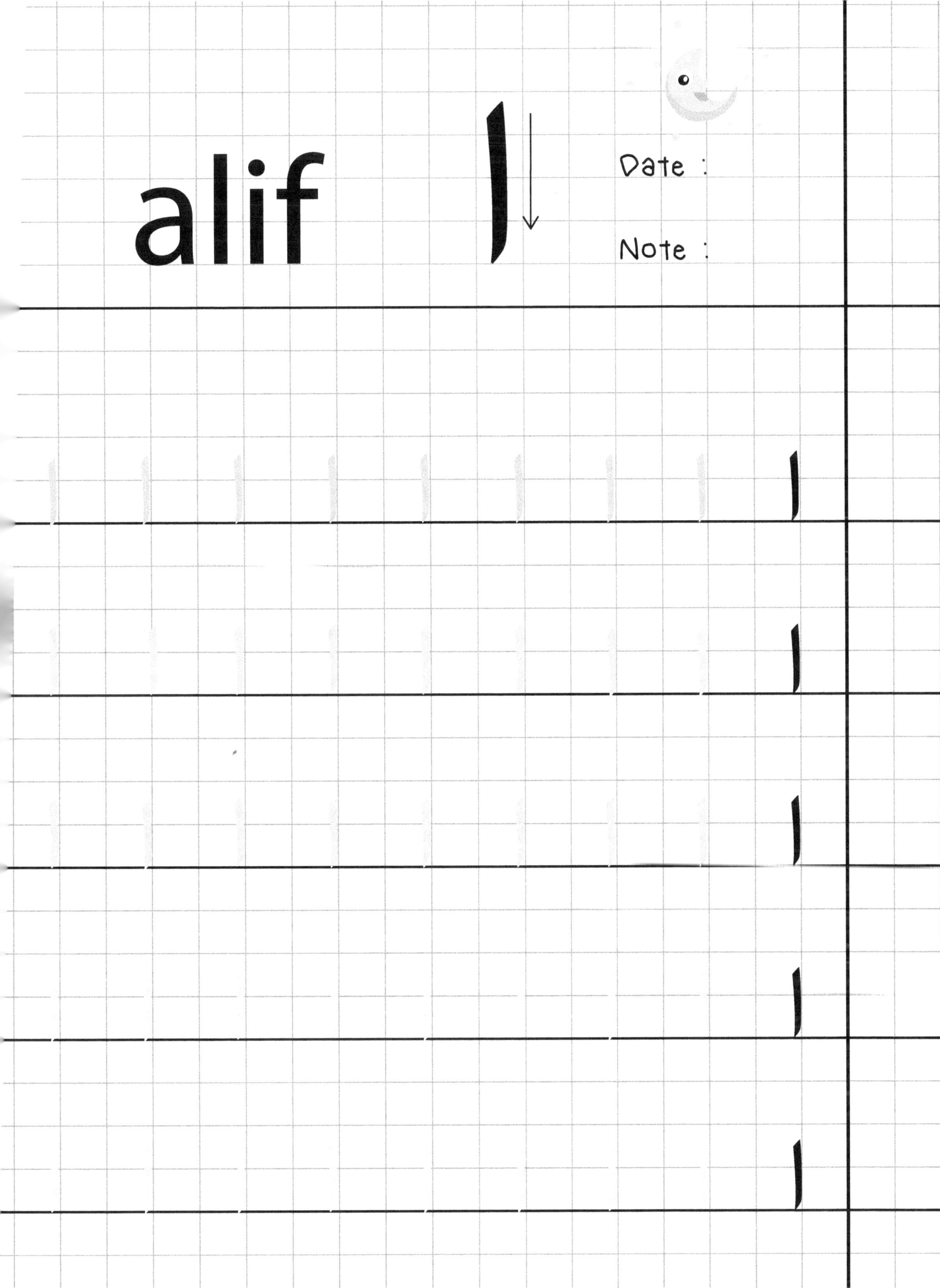

alif

ا

Date :

Note :

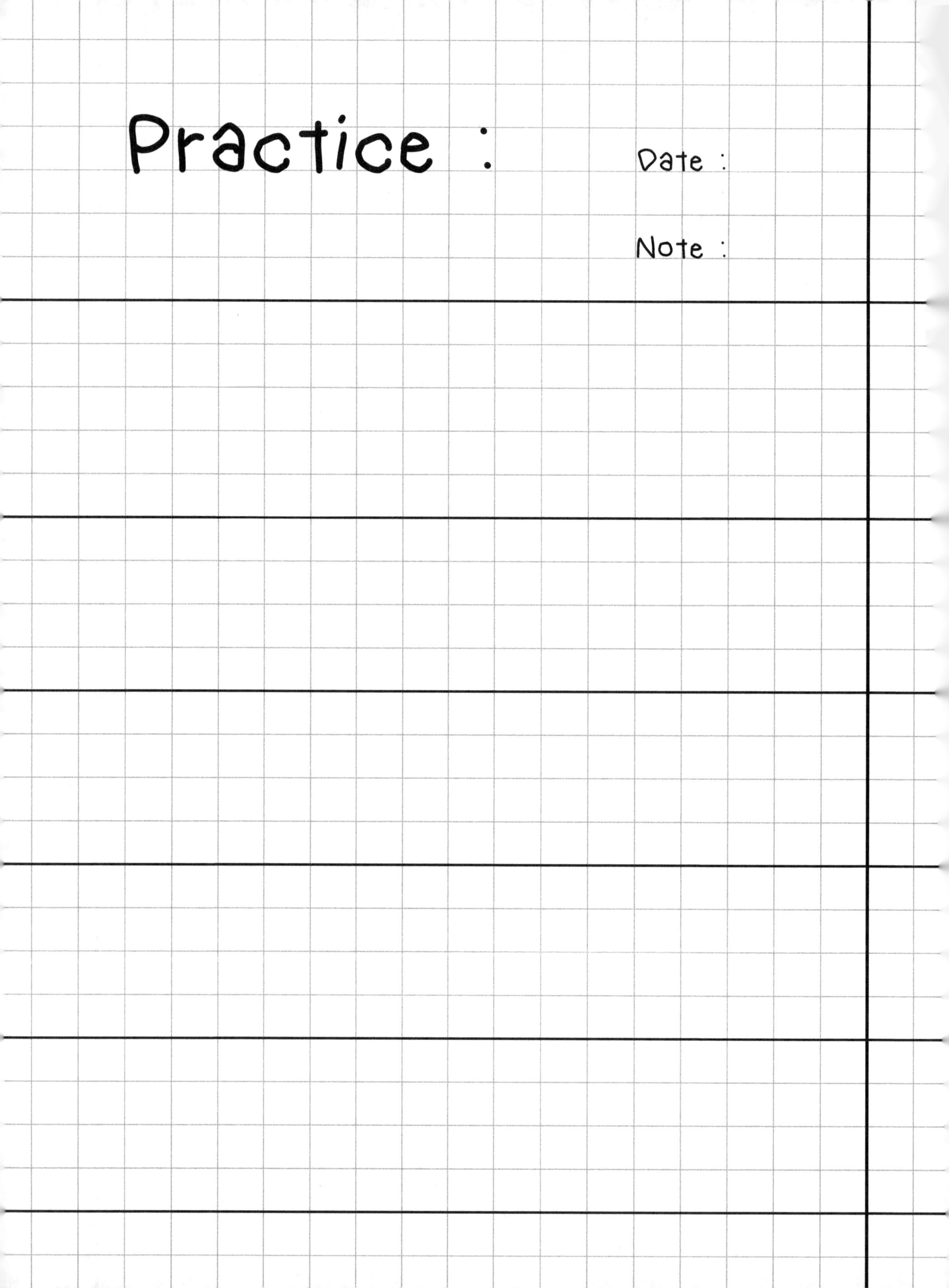

Practice :
Date :
Note :

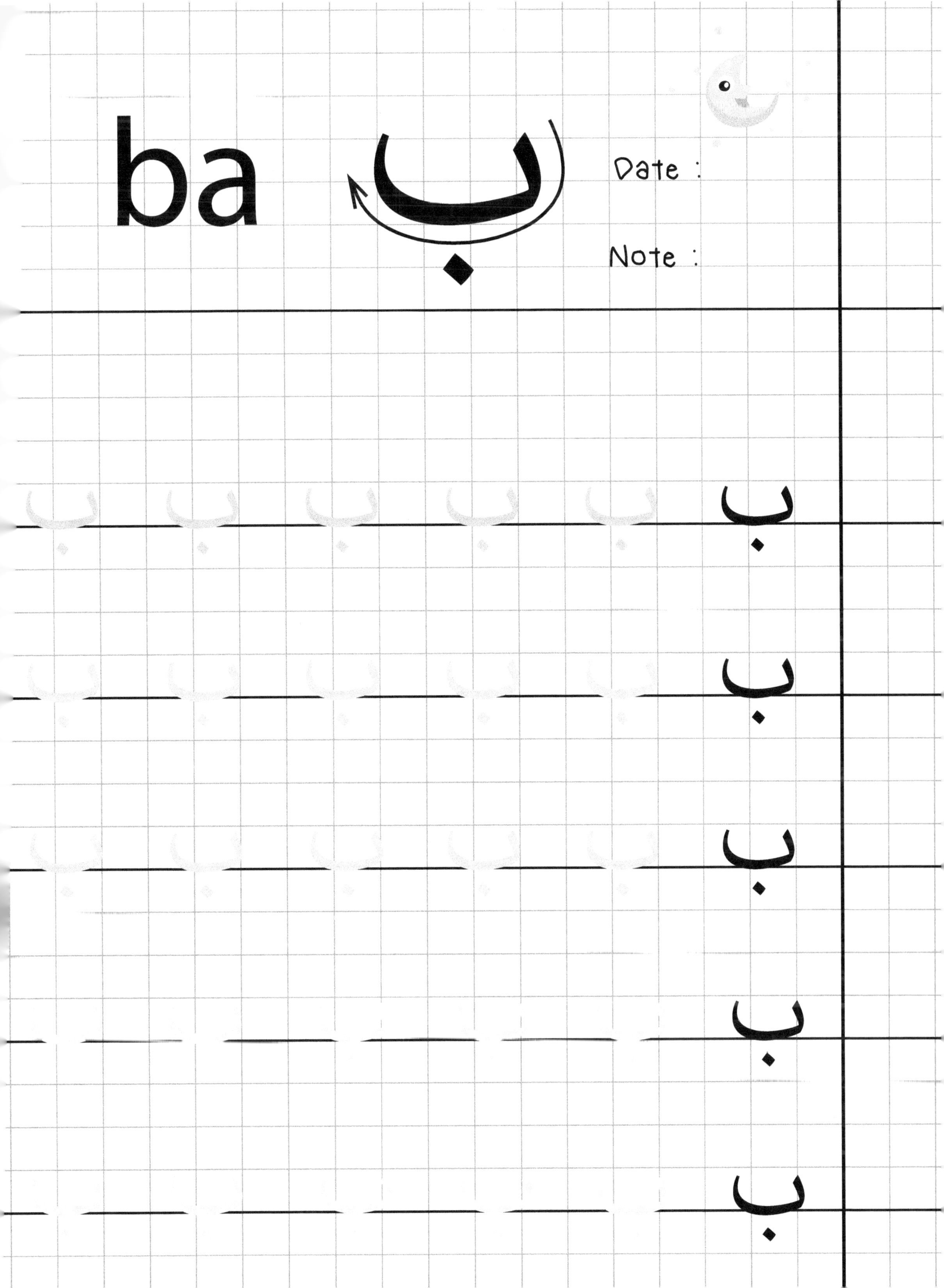

ba ب

Date :

Note :

ب

ب

ب

ب

ب

Practice :

Date :

Note :

ta ت

Date :

Note :

ت

ت

ت

ت

ت

Practice :

Date :

Note :

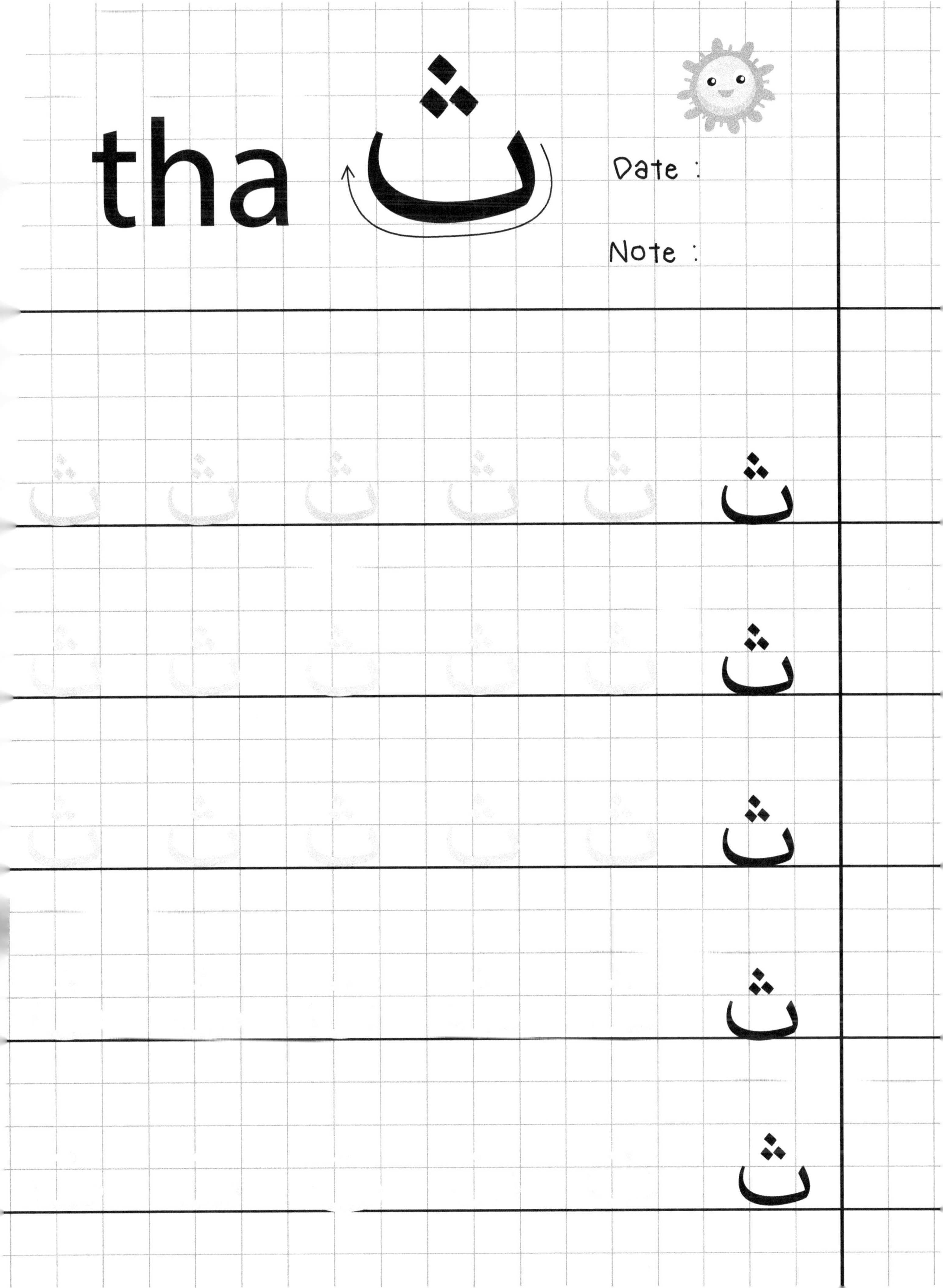

tha ث
Date :
Note :
ث
ث
ث
ث
ث

Practice :

Date :

Note :

jim ج

Date :

Note :

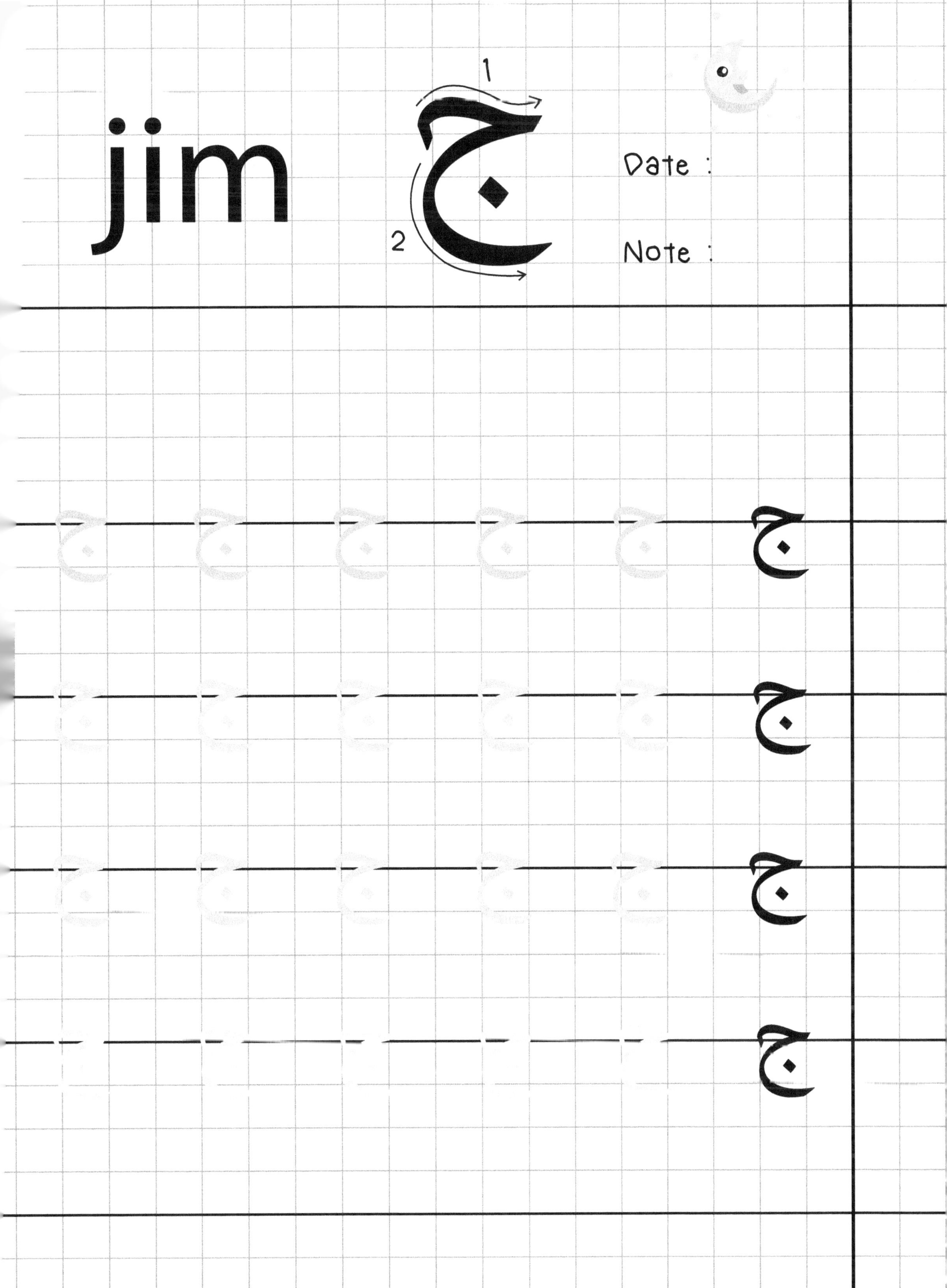

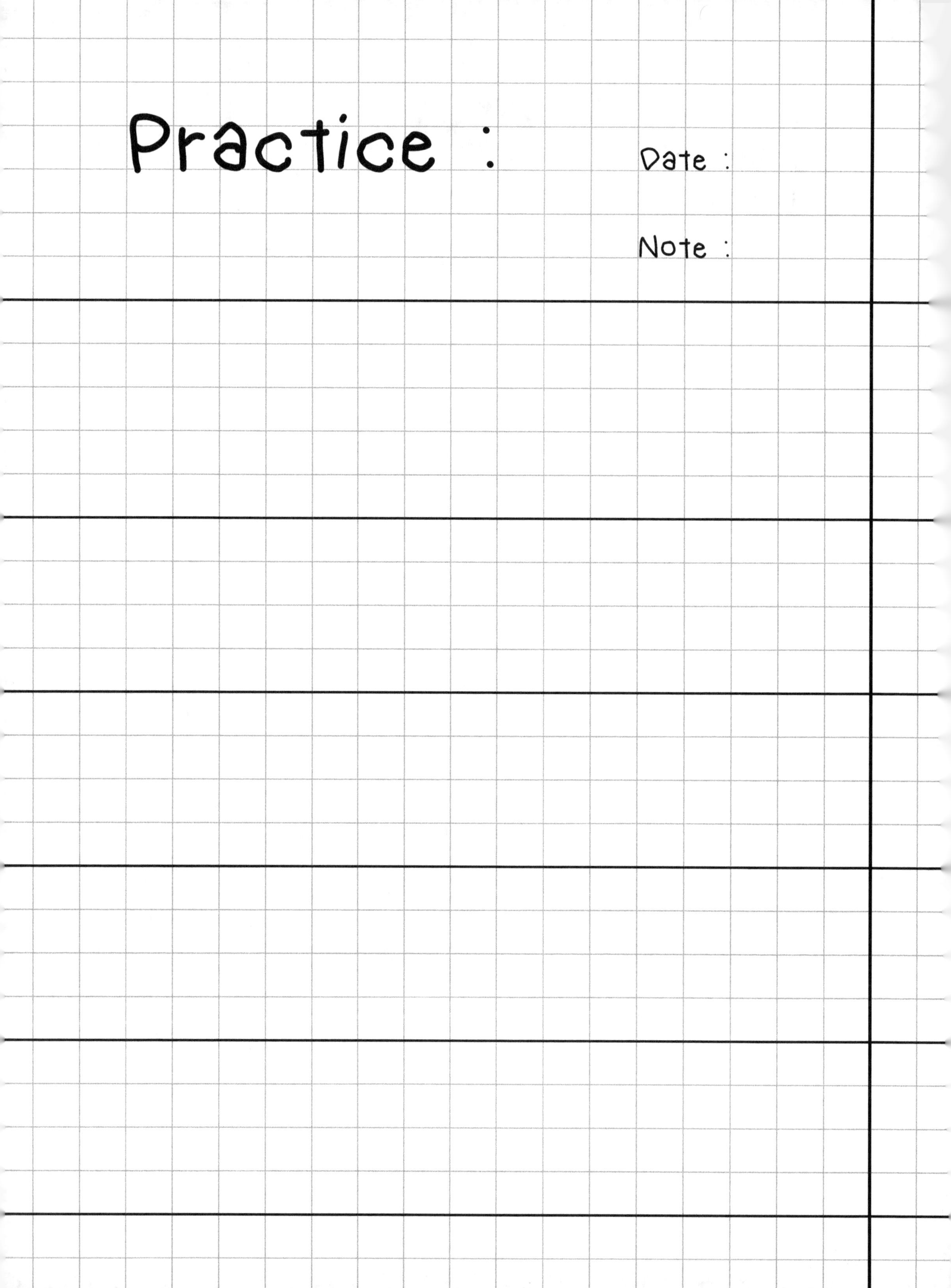

Practice :
Date :
Note :

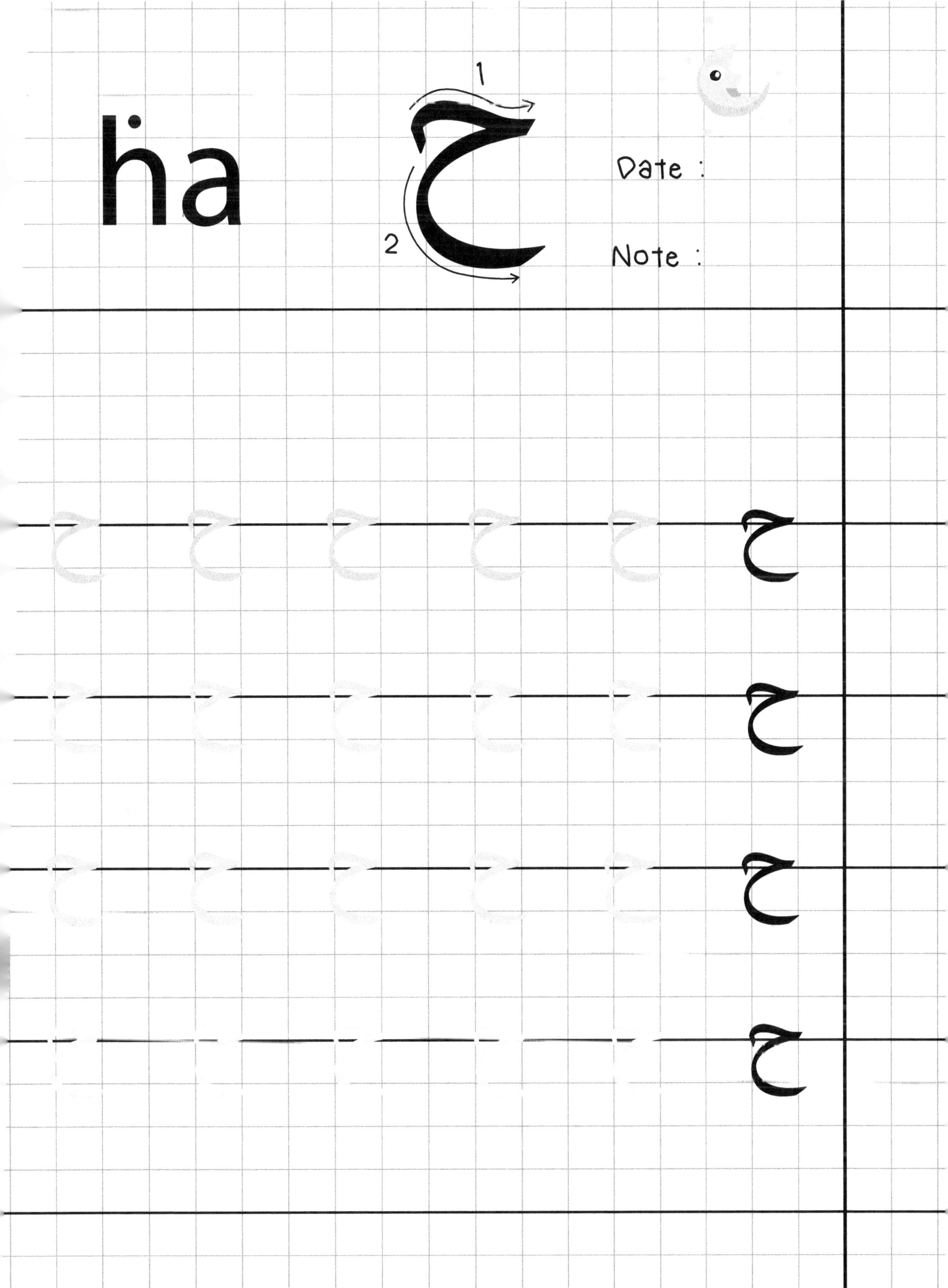
ha
ح
1
2
Date :
Note :

Practice :

Date :

Note :

kha خَ

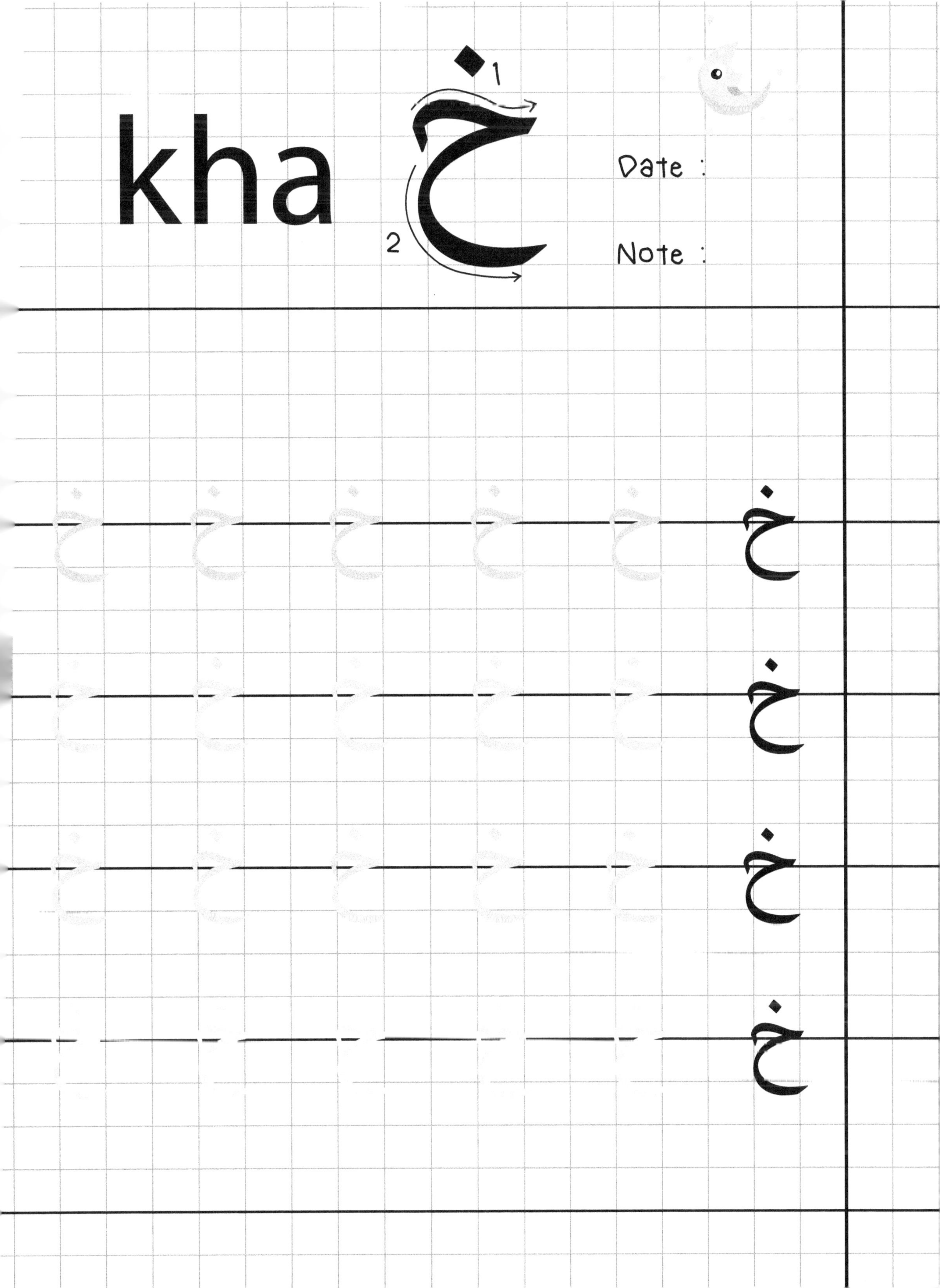

Practice :

Date :

Note :

dal   ﺩ

Date :

Note :

Practice :

Date :

Note :

dhal ذ

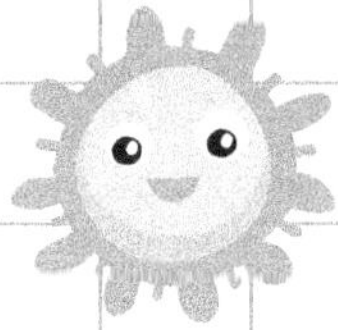

Date :

Note :

ذ ذ ذ ذ ذ ذ ذ ذ ذ

ذ ذ ذ ذ ذ ذ ذ ذ ذ

ذ ذ ذ ذ ذ ذ ذ ذ ذ

ذ

د

Practice :

Date :

Note :

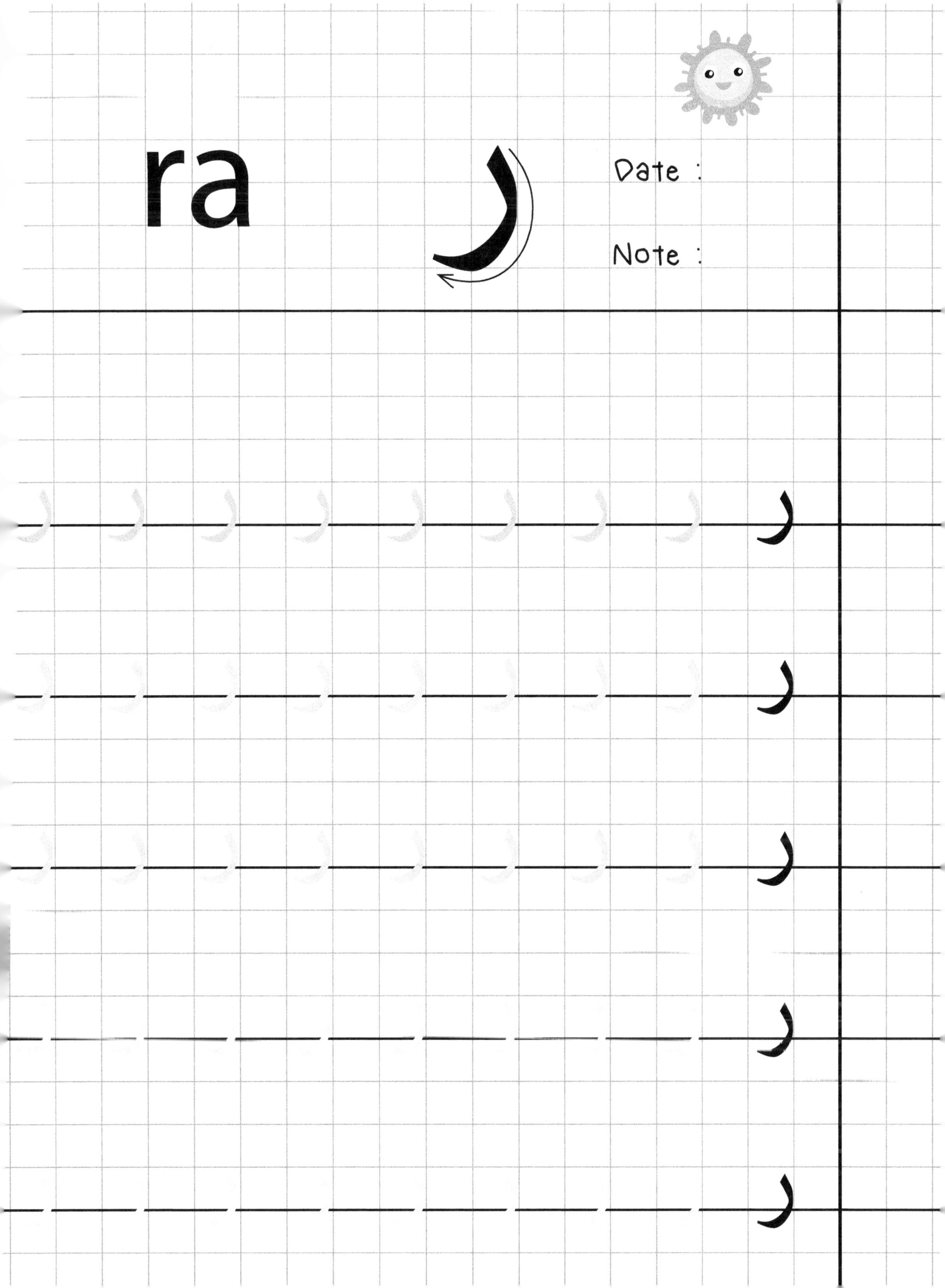
ra
ر
Date :
Note :

Practice :

Date :

Note :

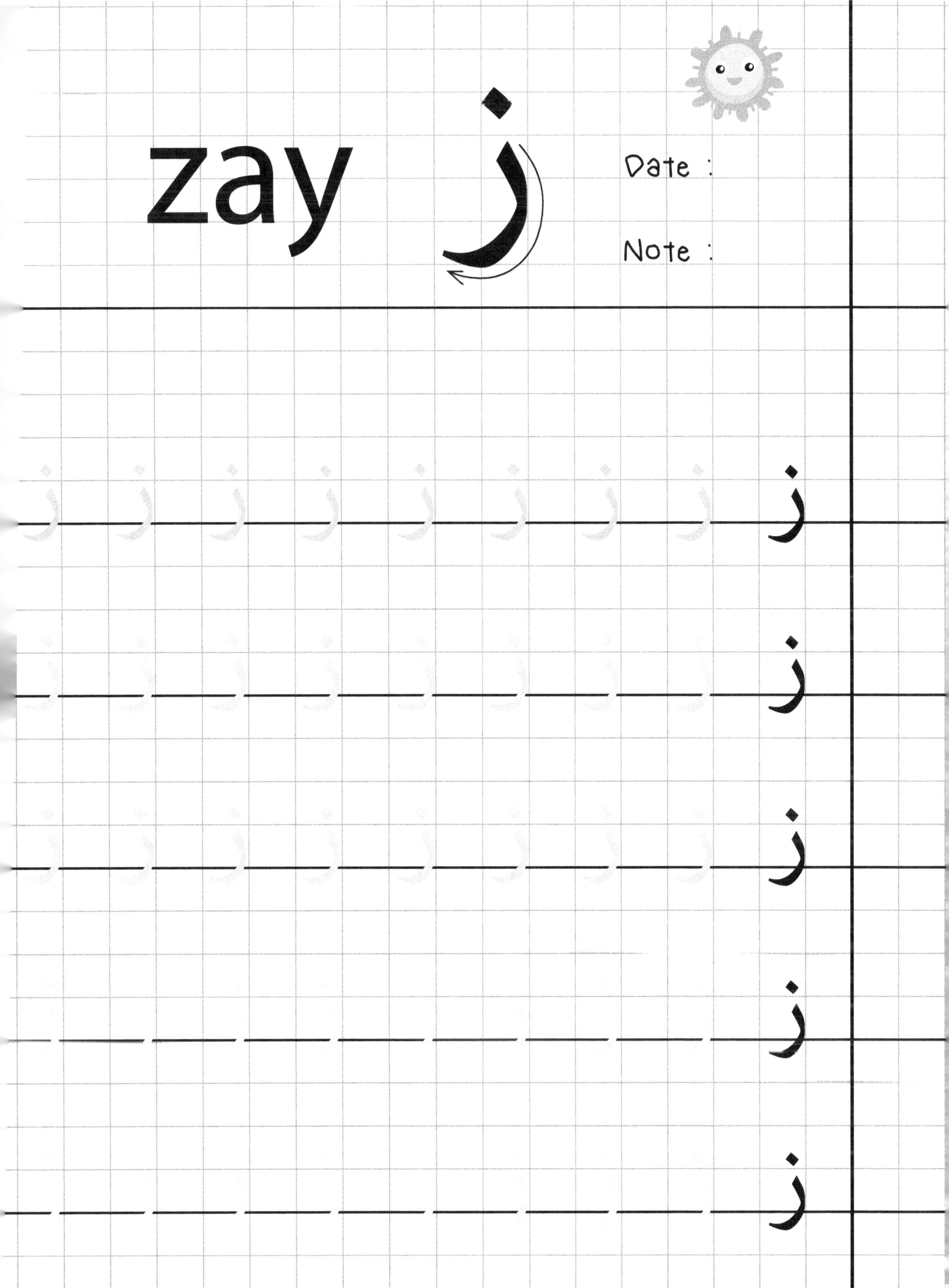

zay ز

Date :

Note :

Practice :

Date :

Note :

sin

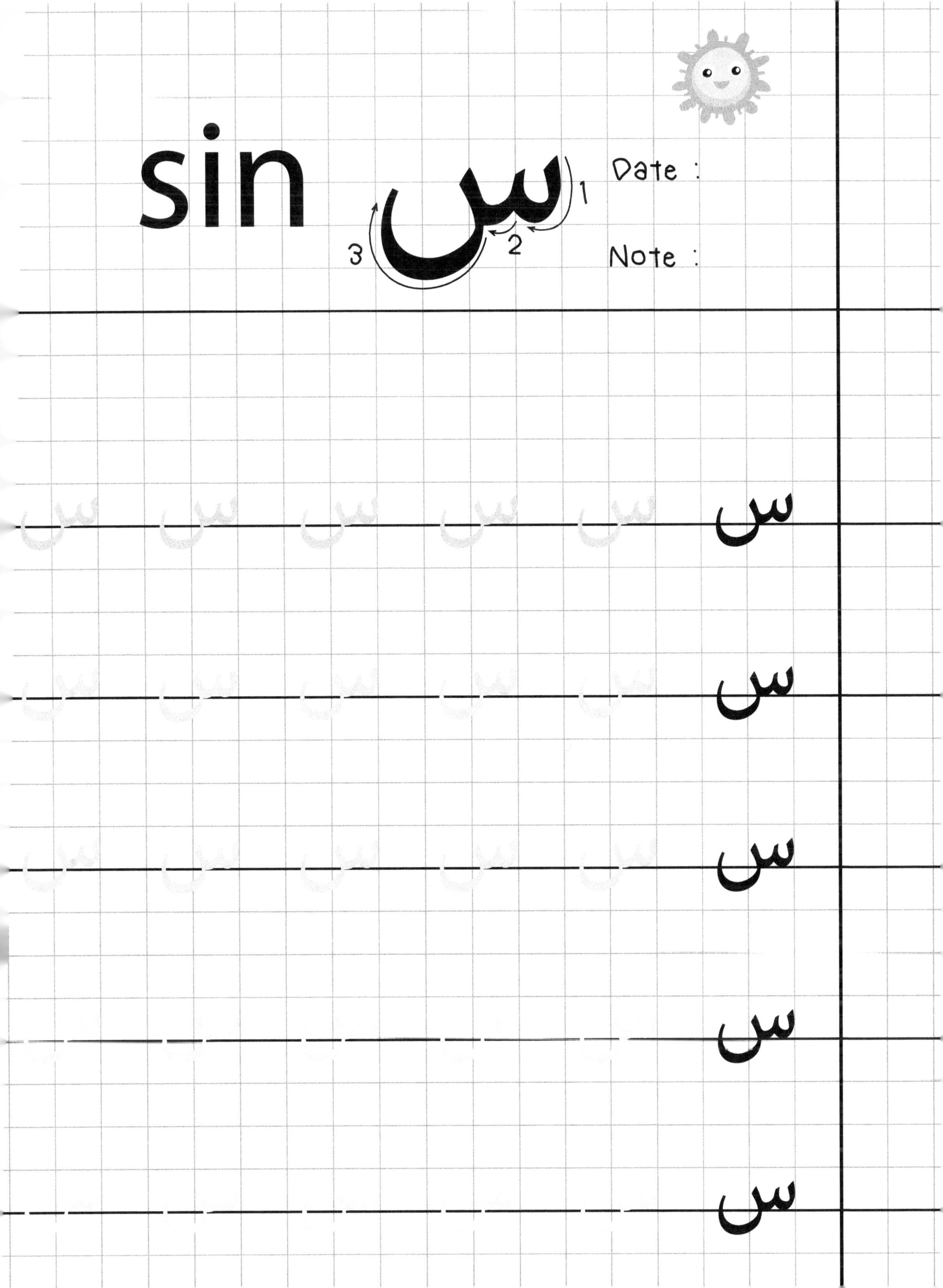

Practice :

Date :

Note :

shin

ش

1

2

3

Date :

Note :

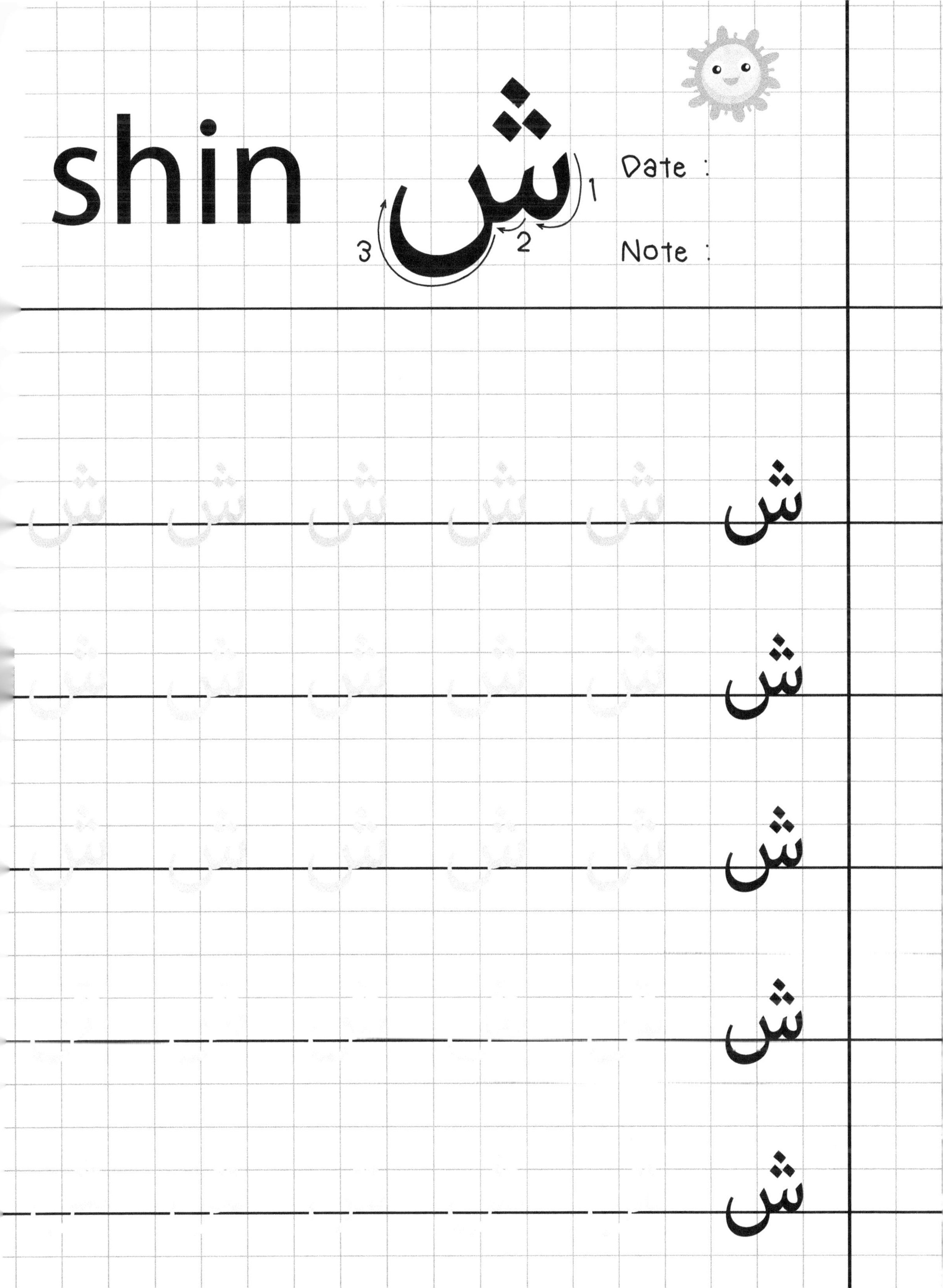

Practice :

Date :

Note :

ṡad

ص

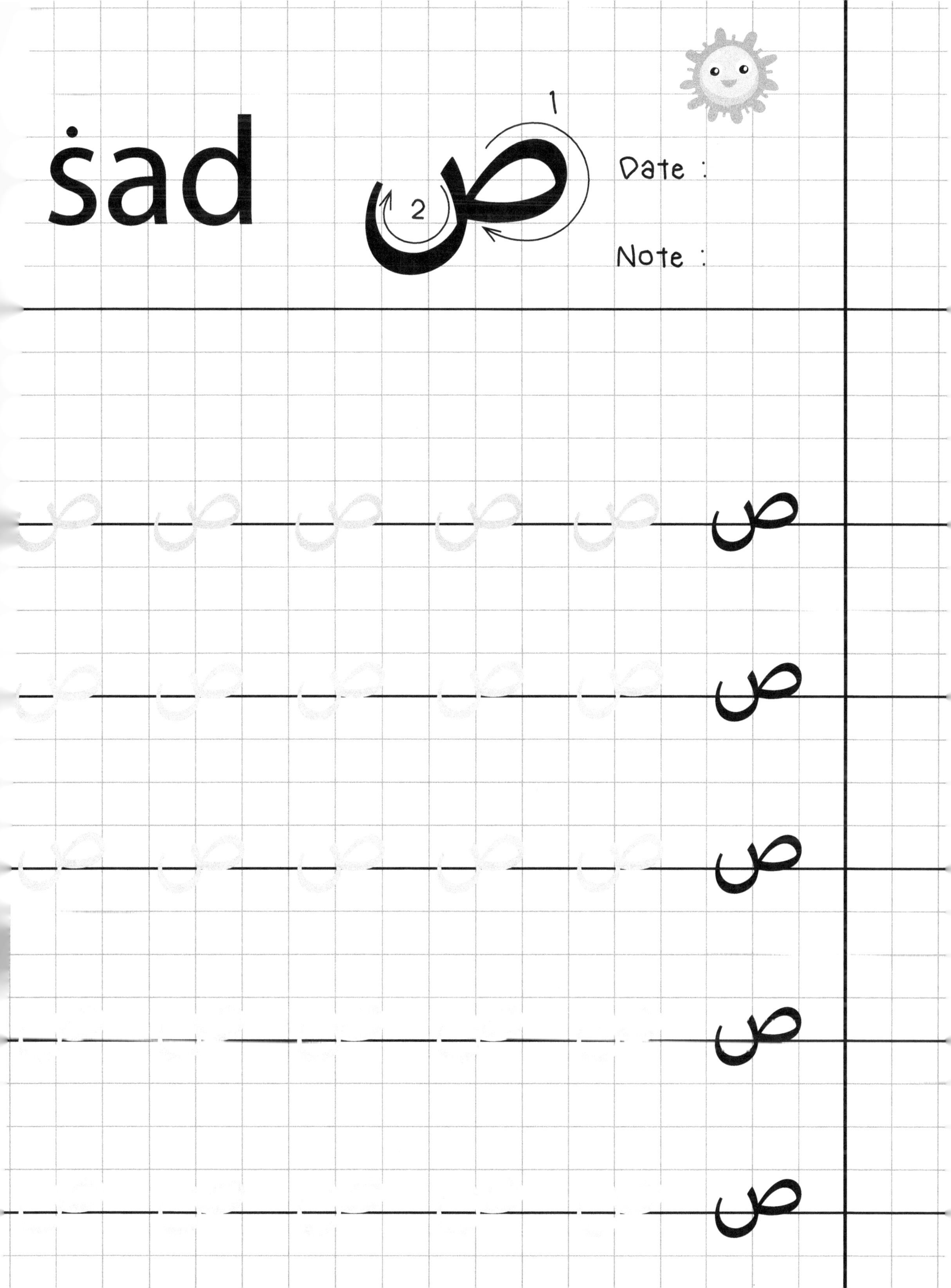

Practice :

Date :

Note :

dad ض

Date :

Note :

ض

ض

ض

ض

ض

Practice :

Date :

Note :

ta

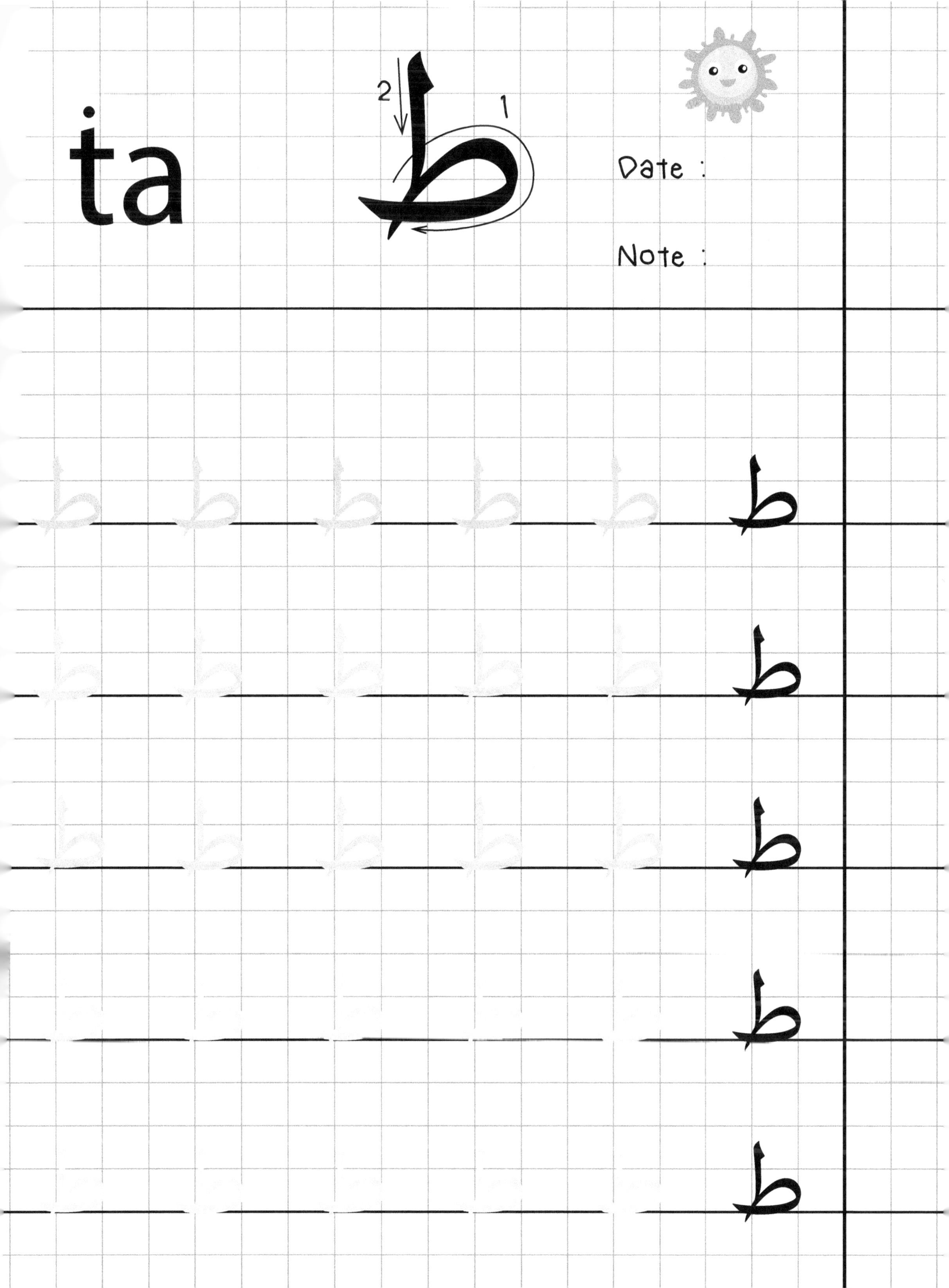

Date :

Note :

ط

ط

ط

ط

ط

Practice :

Date :

Note :

zha ظ
2
1
Date :
Note :
ظ
ظ
ظ
ظ
ظ

Practice :

Date :

Note :

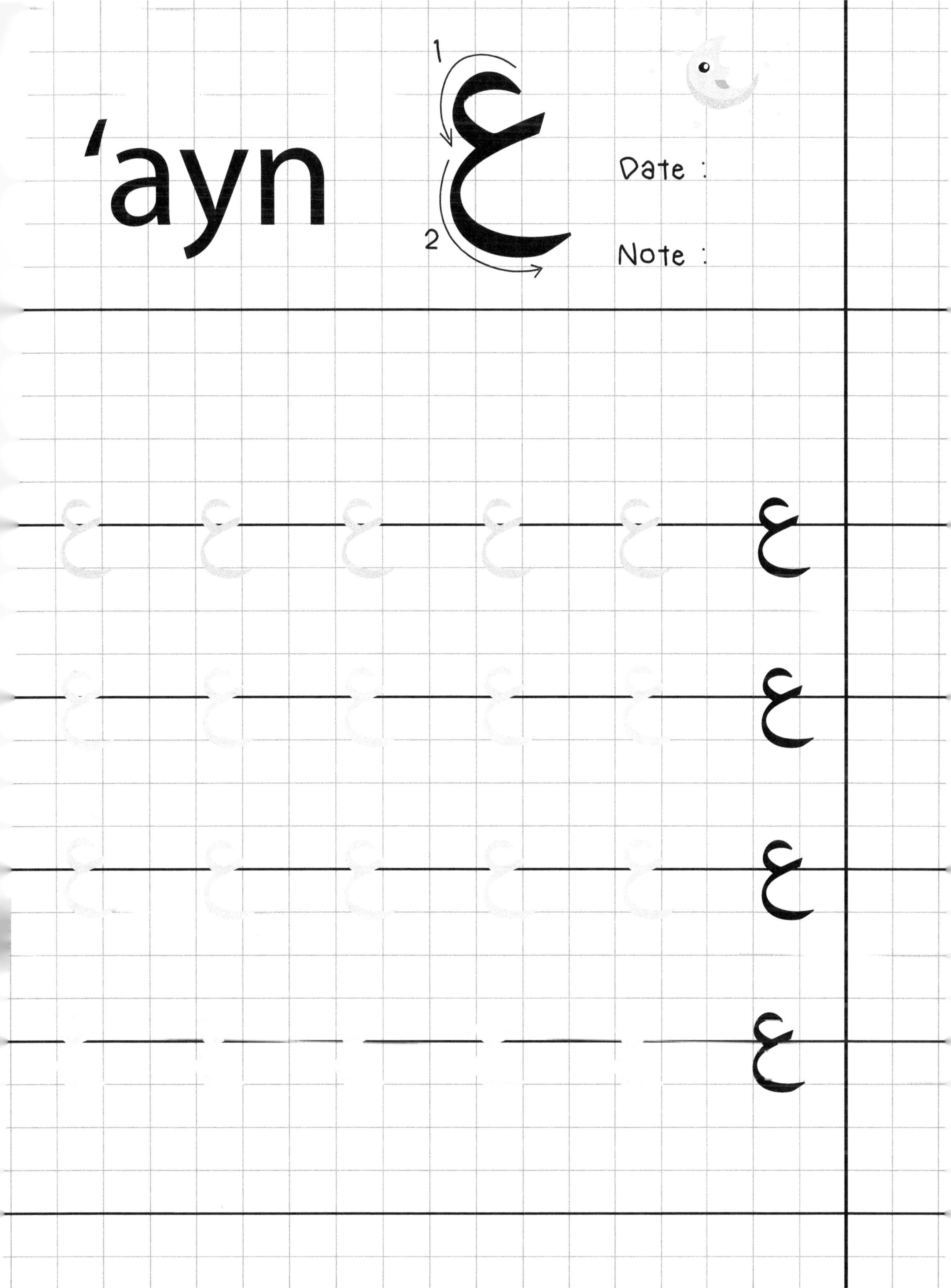
'ayn ع
1
2
Date :
Note :

Practice :

Date :

Note :

ghayn غ

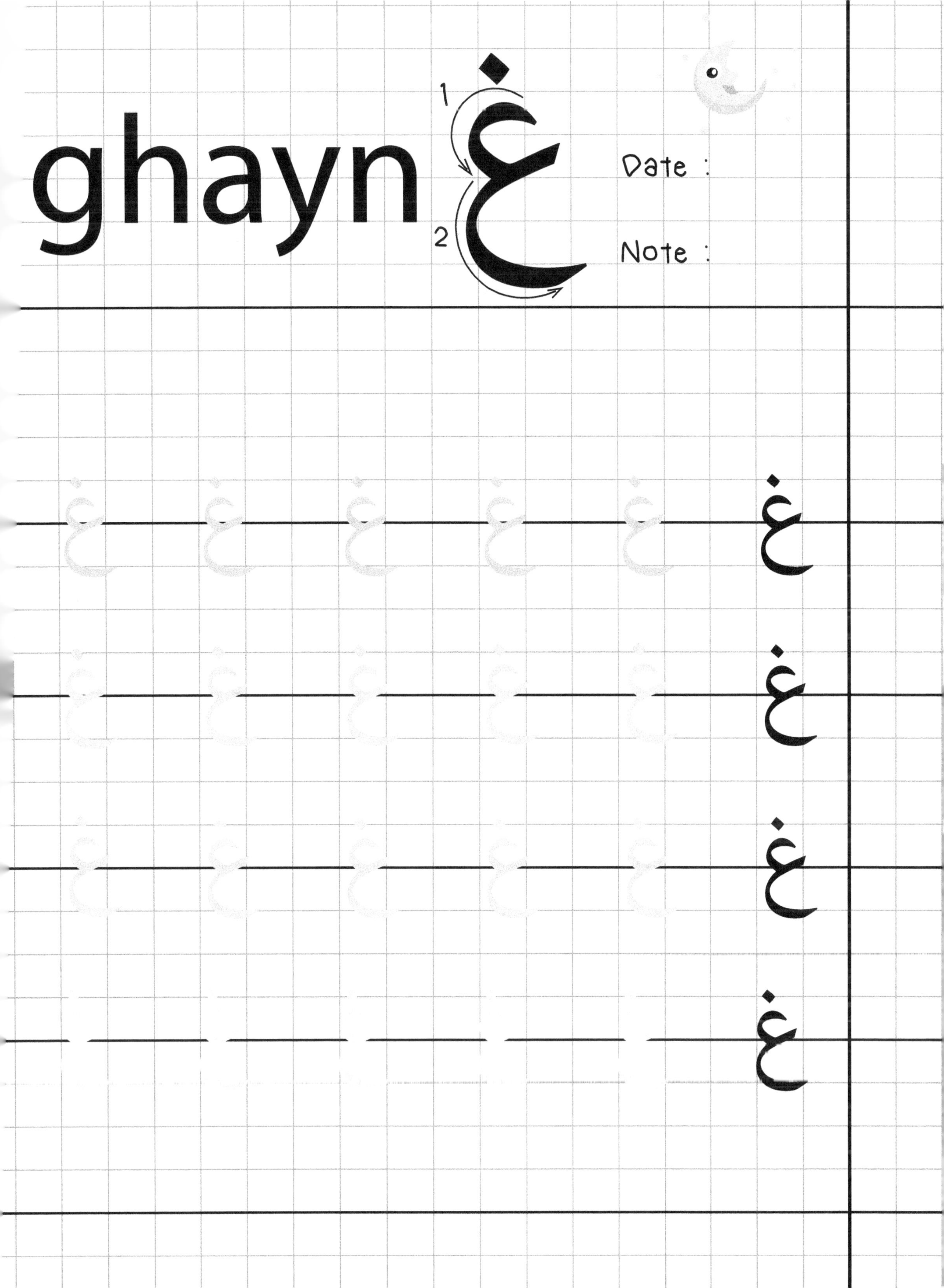

Practice :
Date :
Note :

fa

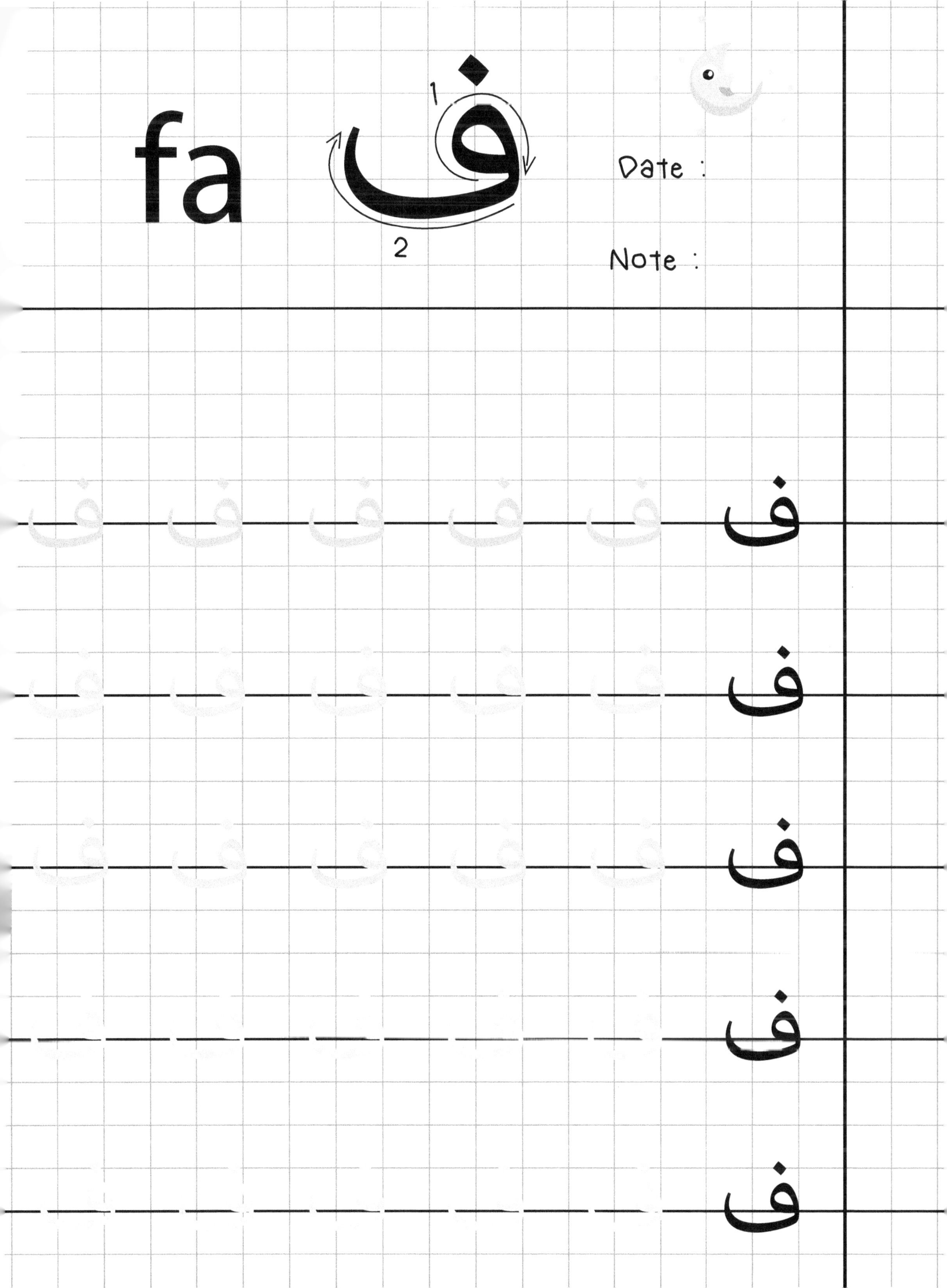

Practice :

Date :

Note :

qaf ق

Date :

Note :

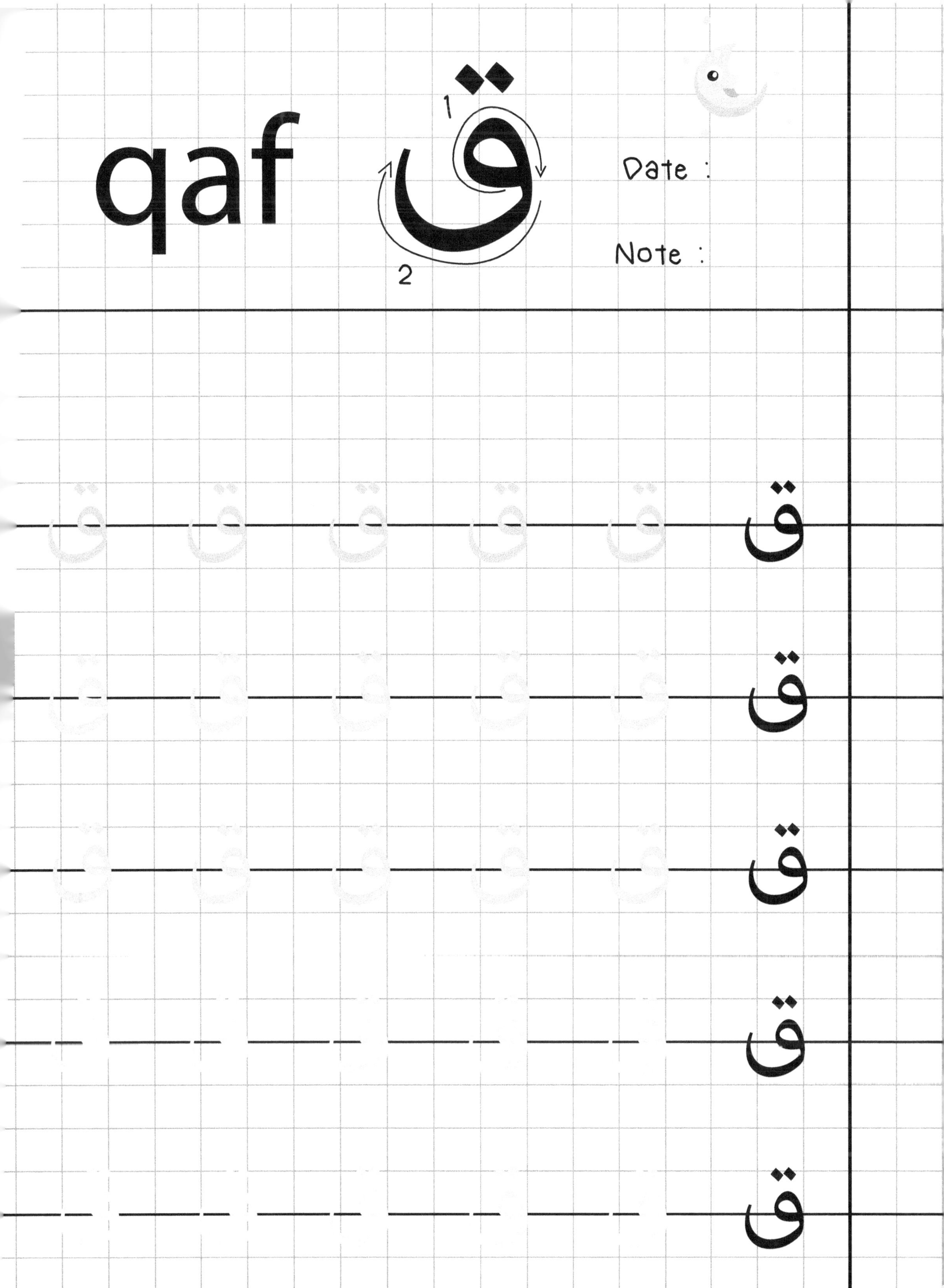

Practice :

Date :

Note :

kaf

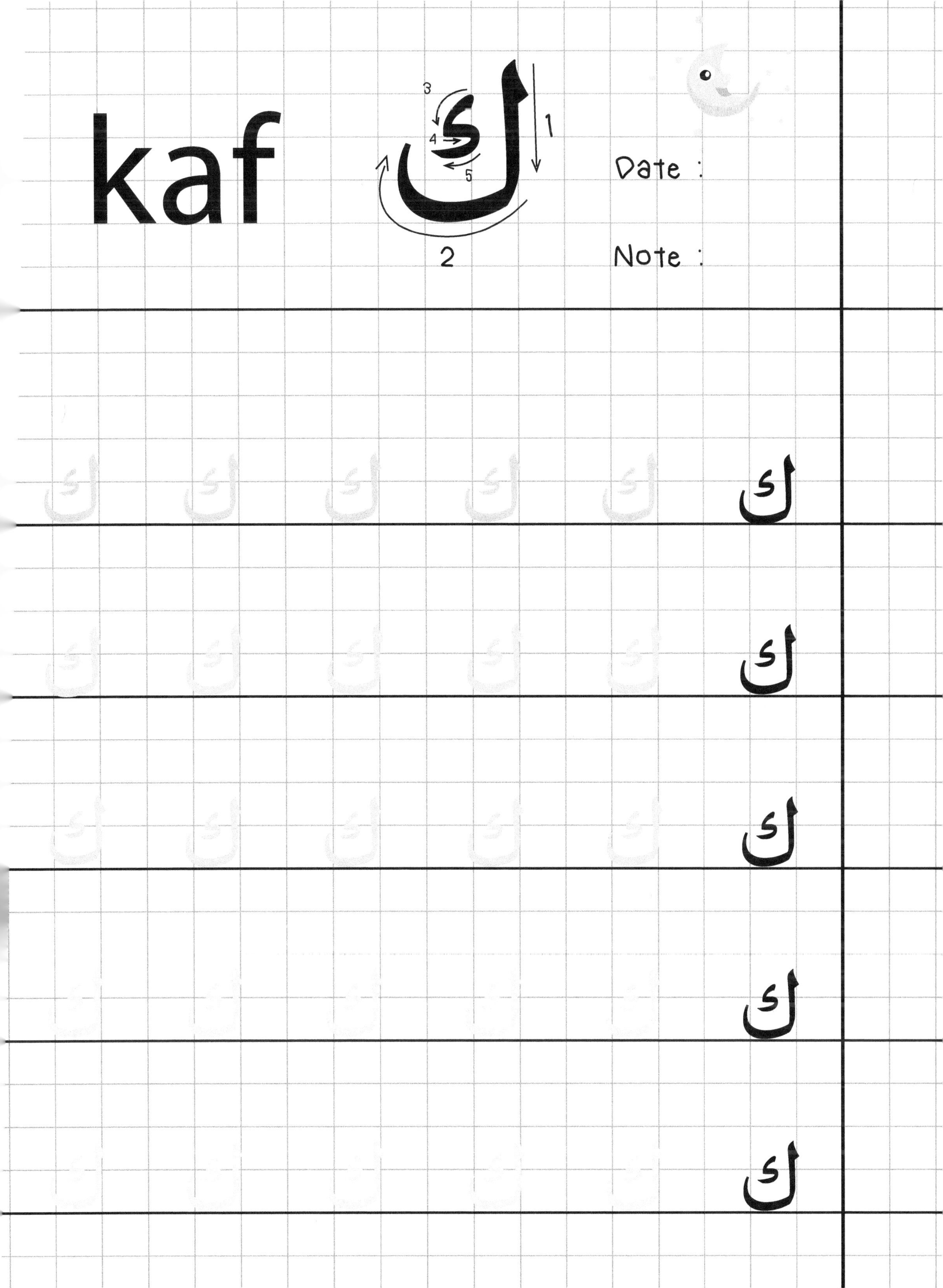

Date :

Note :

ك

ك

ك

ك

ك

Practice :

Date :

Note :

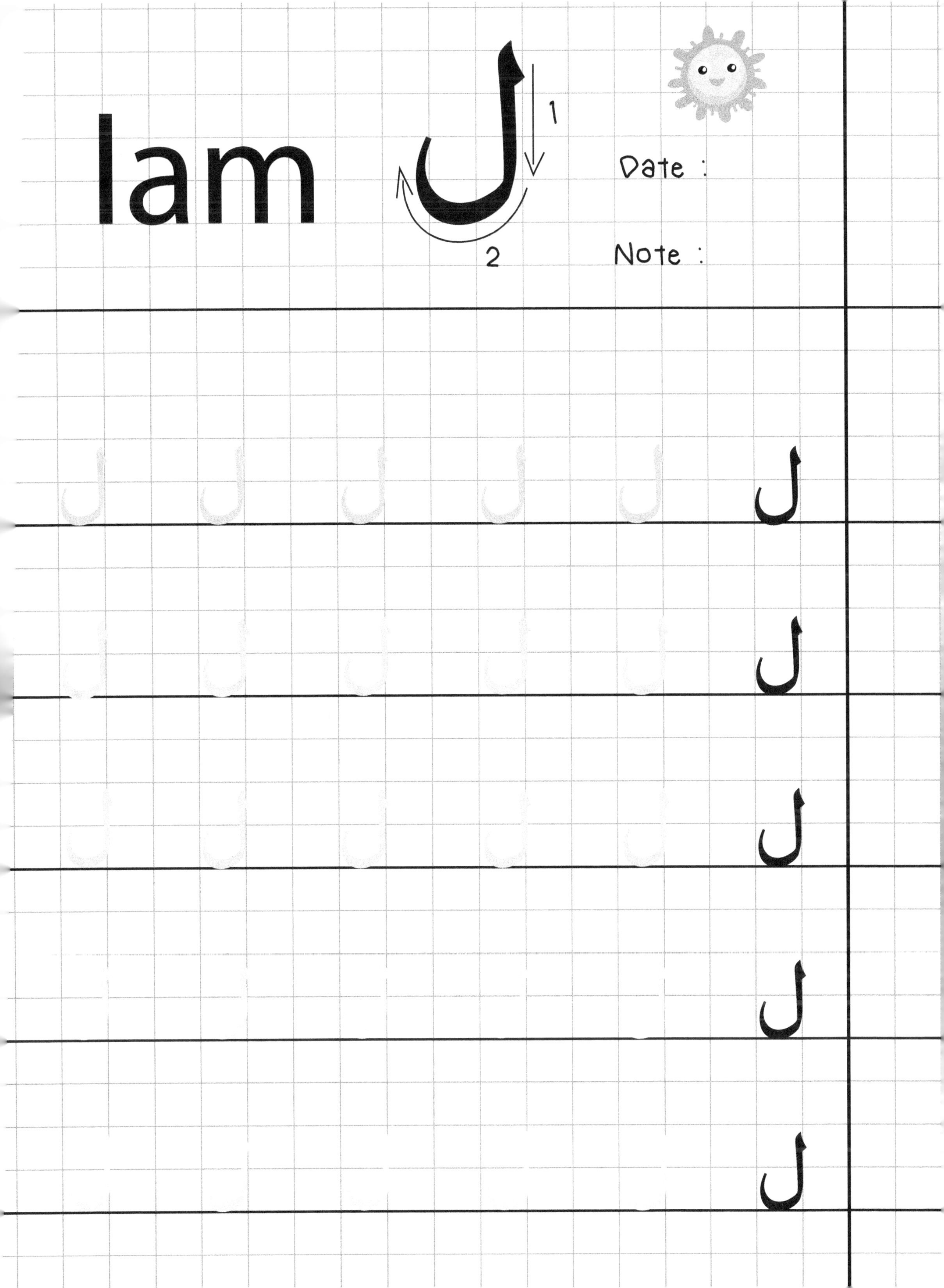

lam   ل

Date :

Note :

Practice :

Date :

Note :

mim

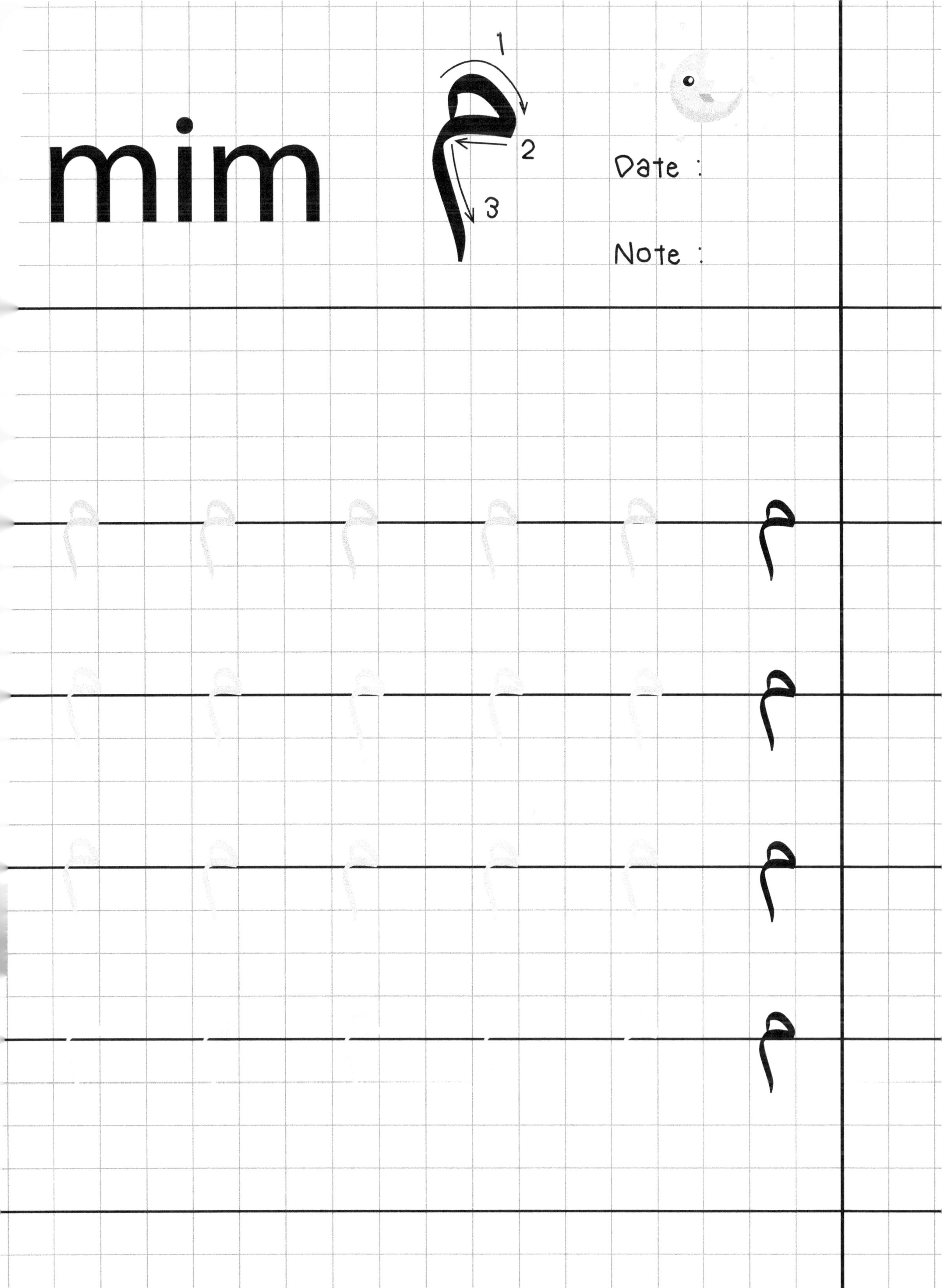

Practice :

Date :

Note :

nun ن

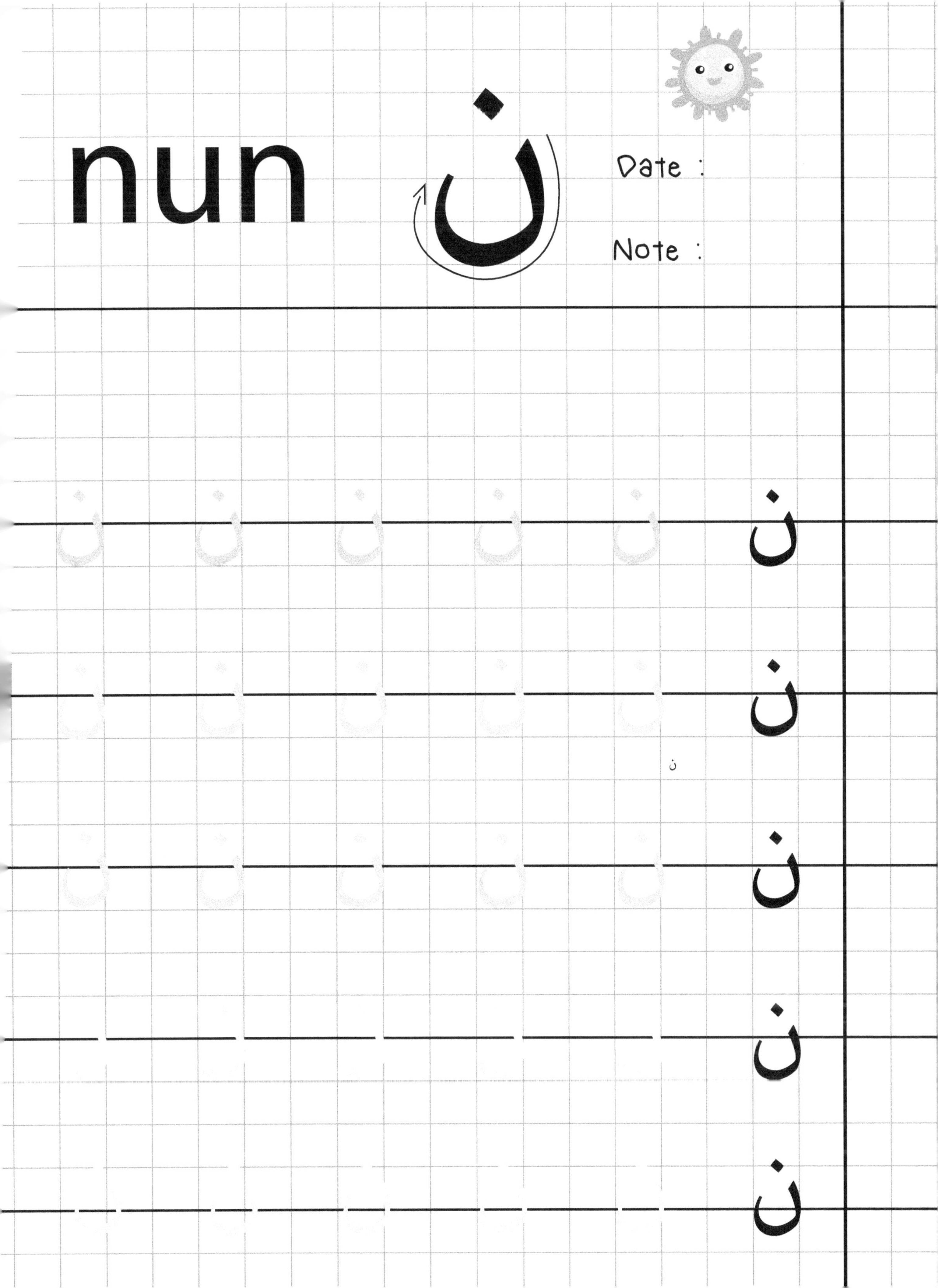

Date :

Note :

ن

ن

ن

ن

ن

Practice :

Date :

Note :

waw

					و
					و
					و
					و
					و

Practice :

Date :

Note :

ha

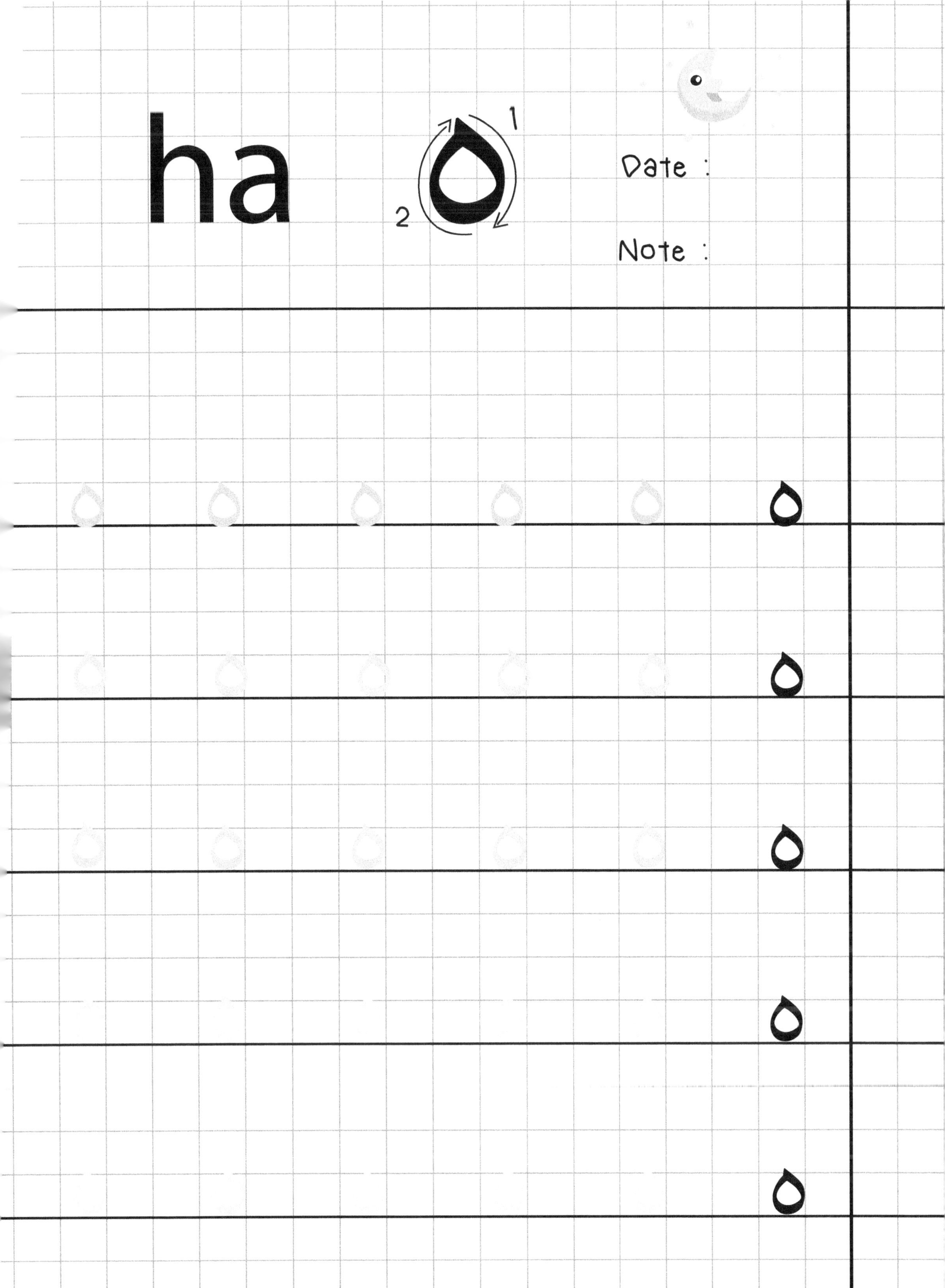

Practice :

Date :

Note :

ya ــيــ

Date :

Note :

ي

ي

ي

ي

Practice :

Date :

Note :

hamza 

Practice :   Date :

                          Note :

Practice :

Date :

Note :

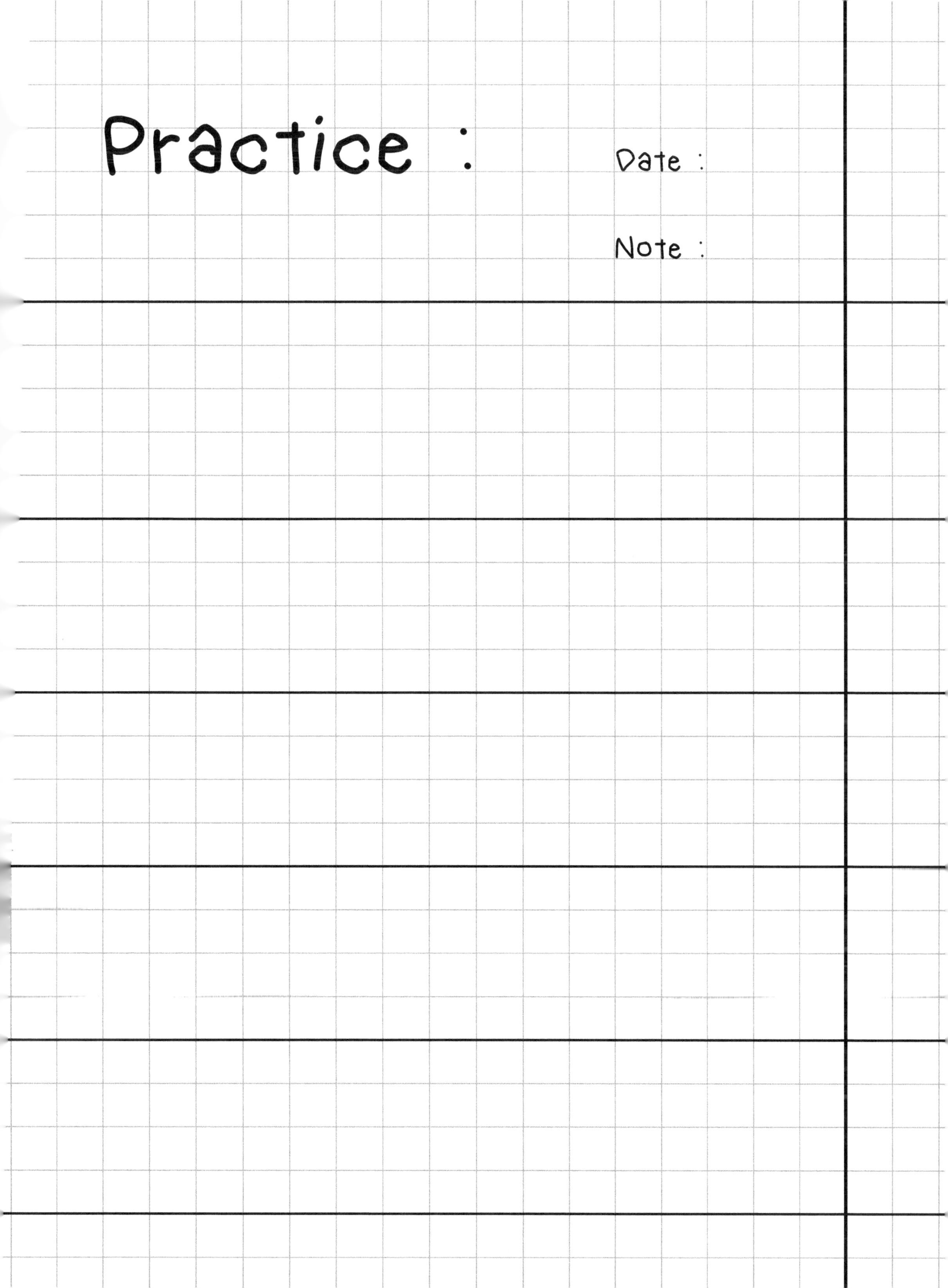

Practice :

Date :

Note :

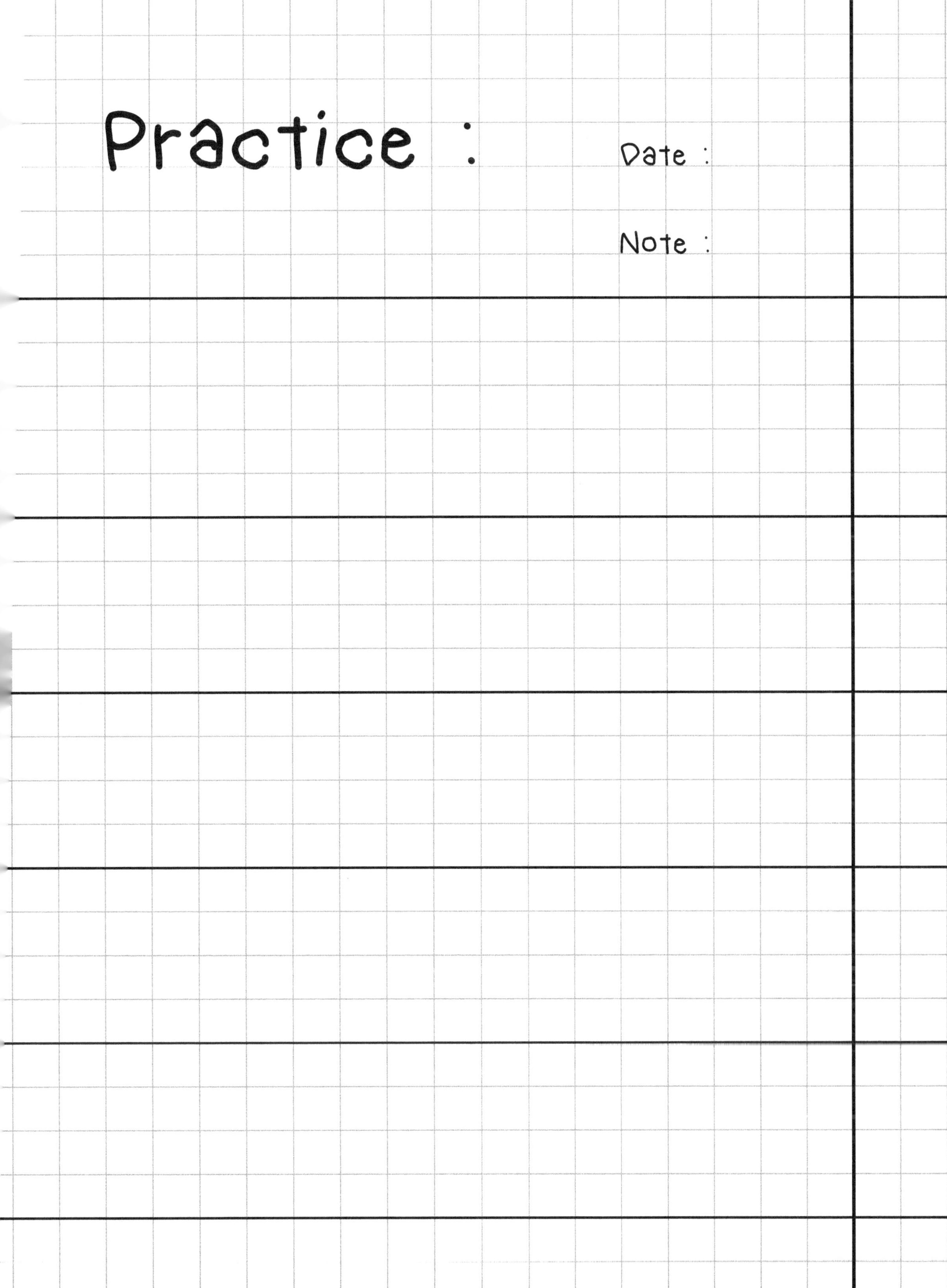
Practice :
Date :
Note :

Practice :

Date :

Note :

Practice :

Date :

Note :

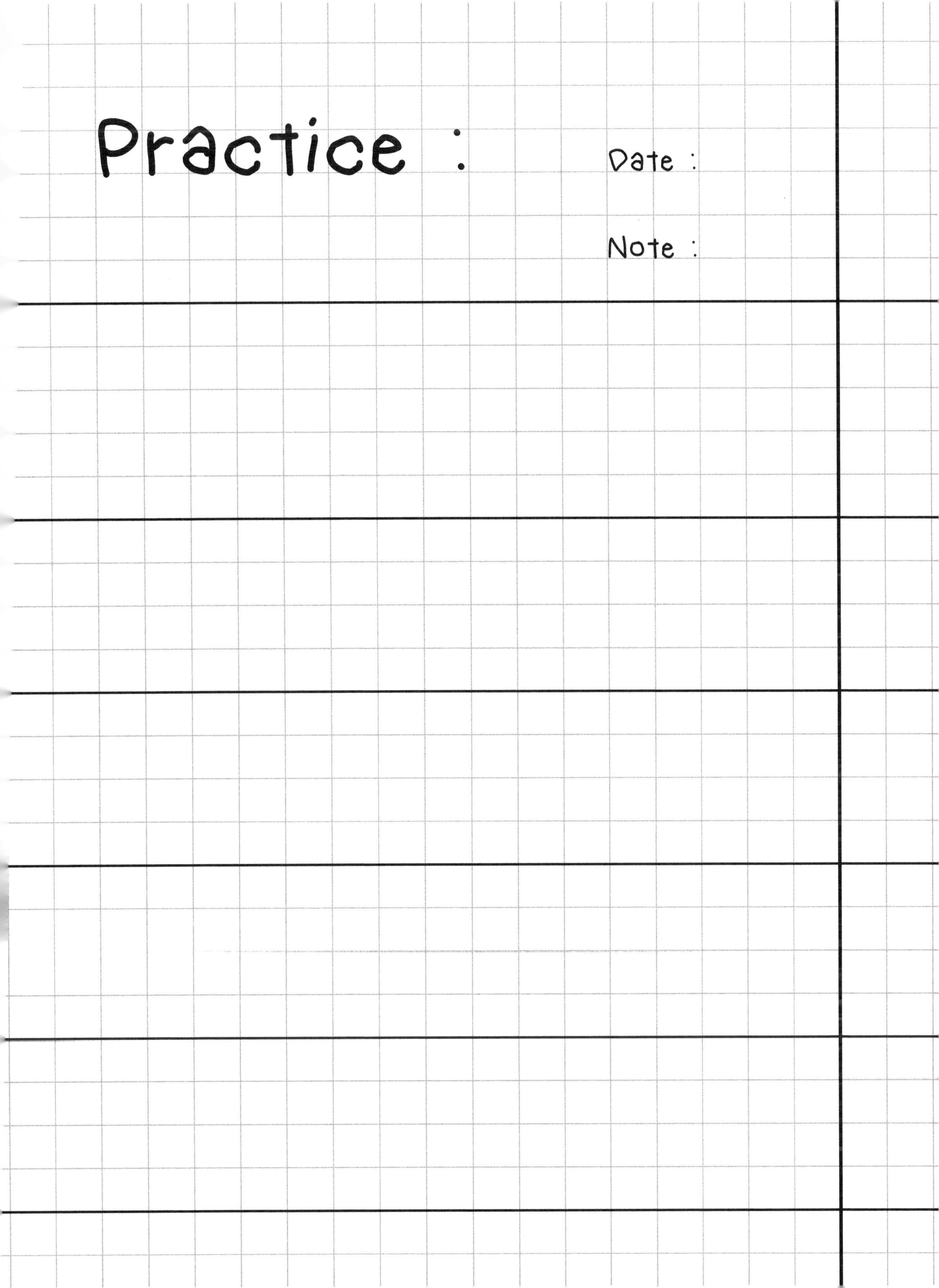

Practice :

Date :

Note :

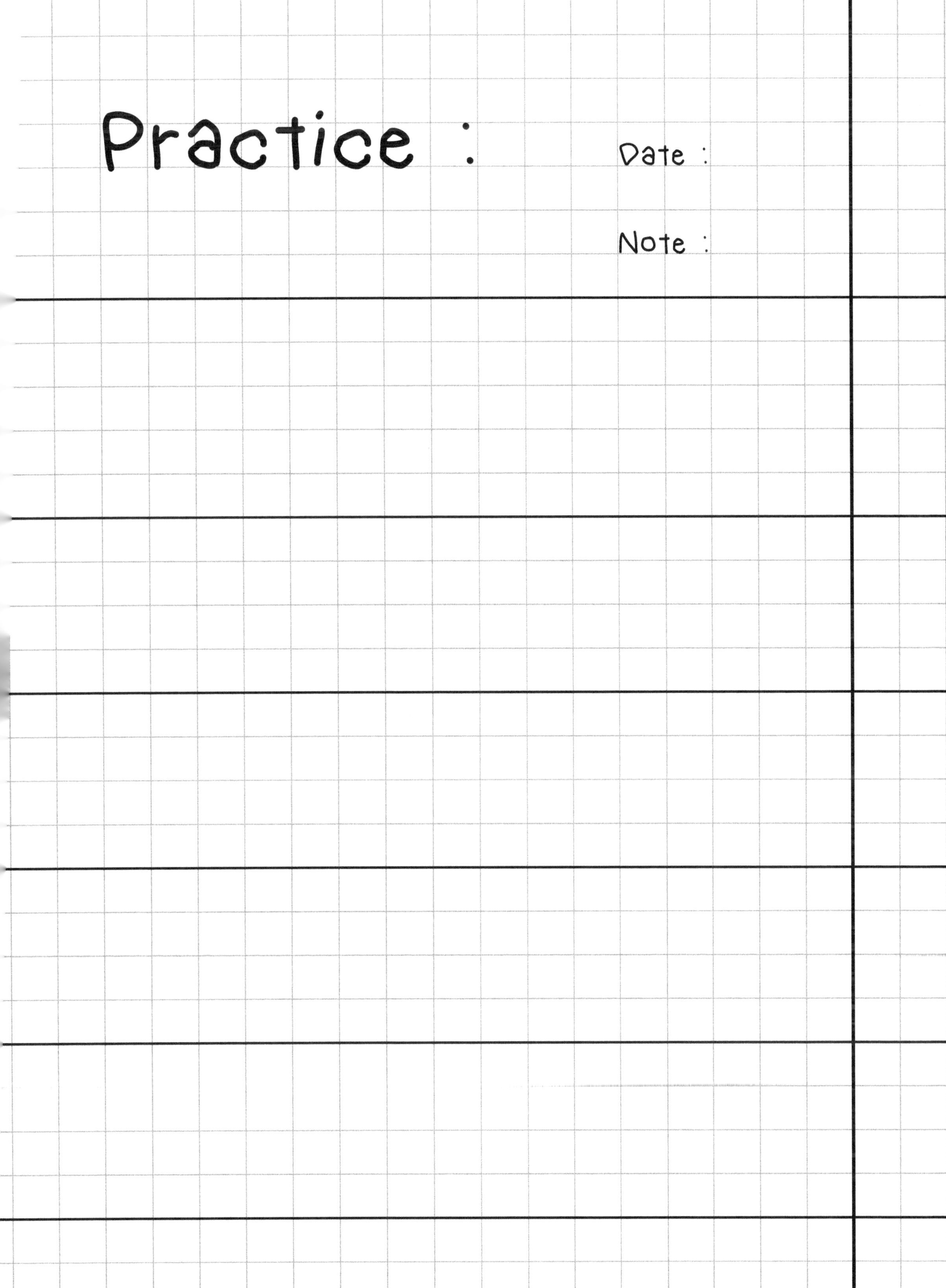

Practice :
Date :
Note :

Practice :

Date :

Note :

Practice :

Date :

Note :

Practice :   Date :

Note :

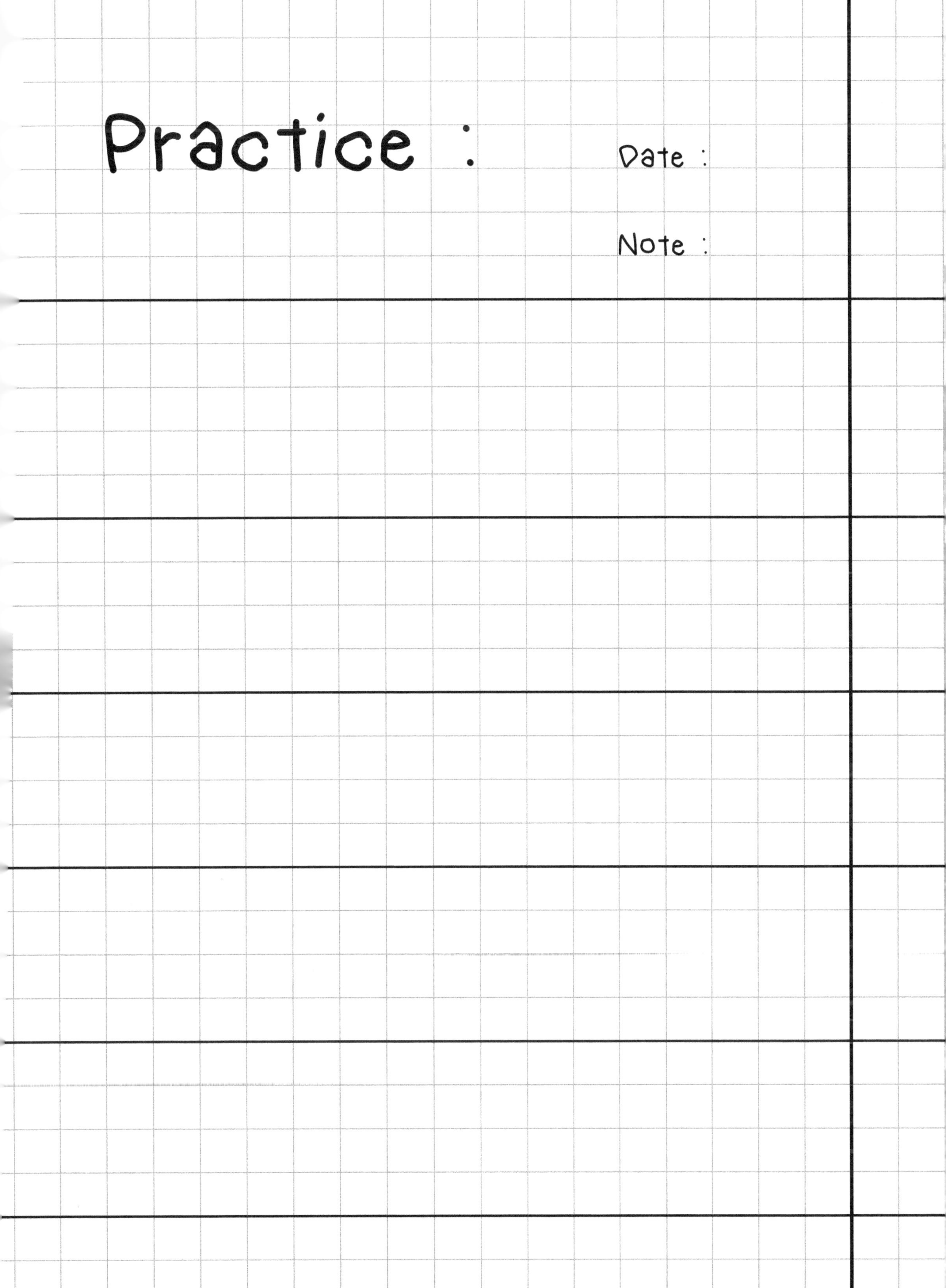

Practice :
Date :
Note :

Practice :

Date :

Note :

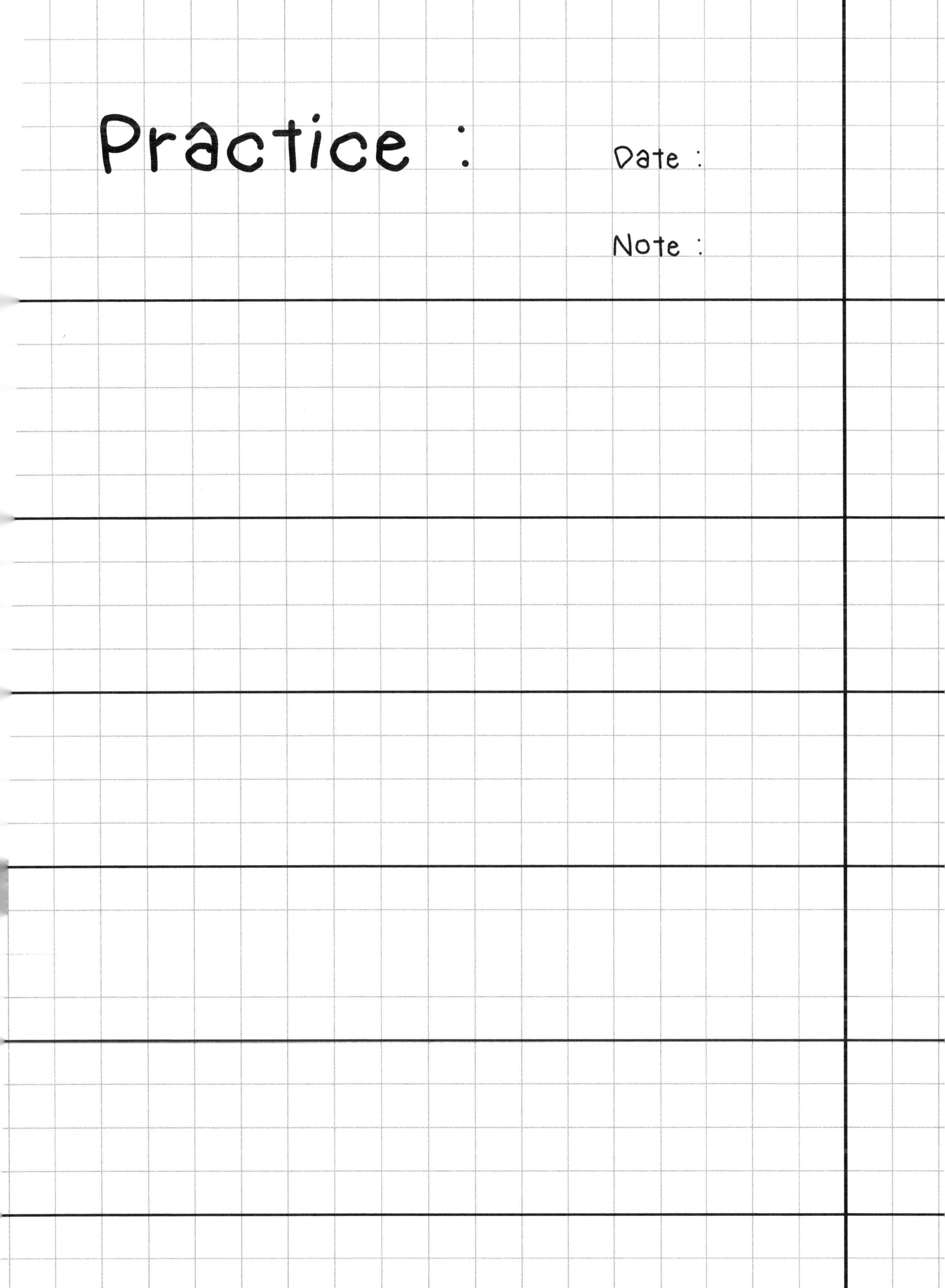

Practice :
Date :
Note :

Practice :

Date :

Note :

Practice :
Date :
Note :

Practice :

Date :

Note :

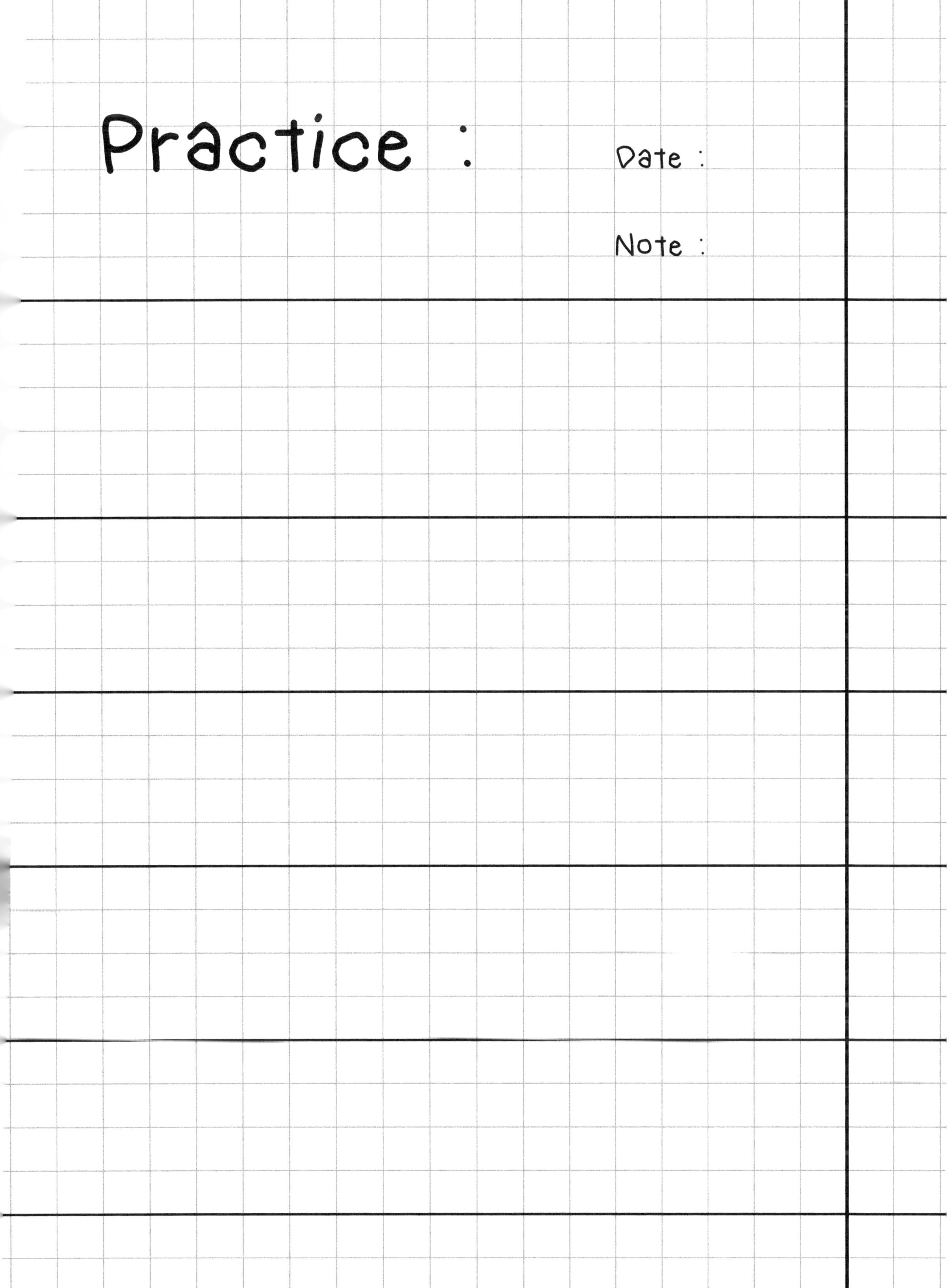
Practice :
Date :
Note :

Practice :

Date :

Note :

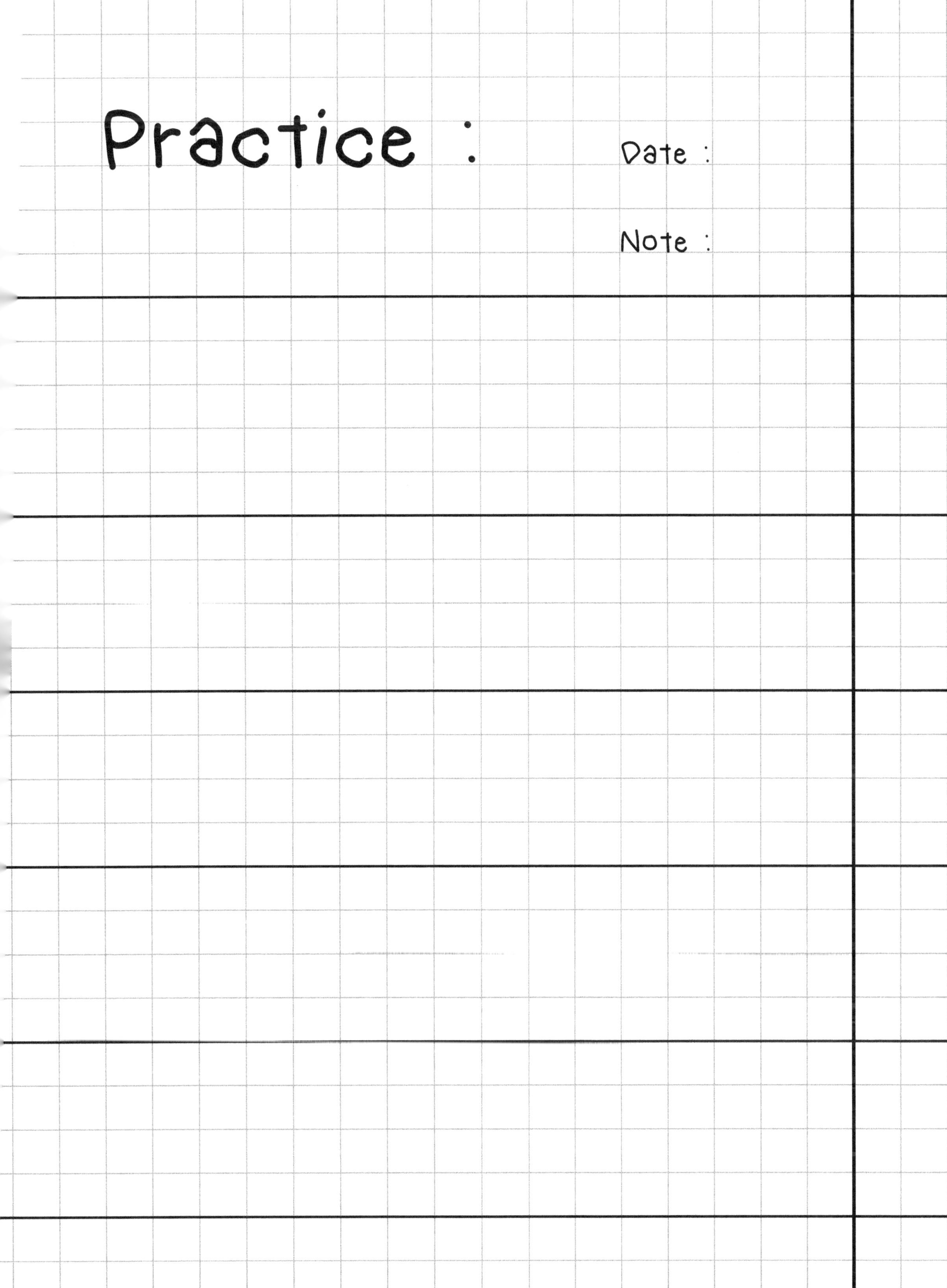

Practice :
Date :
Note :

Practice :

Date :

Note :

Practice :

Date :

Note :

Practice :

Date :

Note :

Practice :
Date :
Note :

Practice :

Date :

Note :

Practice :

Date :

Note :

Practice :

Date :

Note :

Practice :
Date :
Note :

Practice :

Date :

Note :

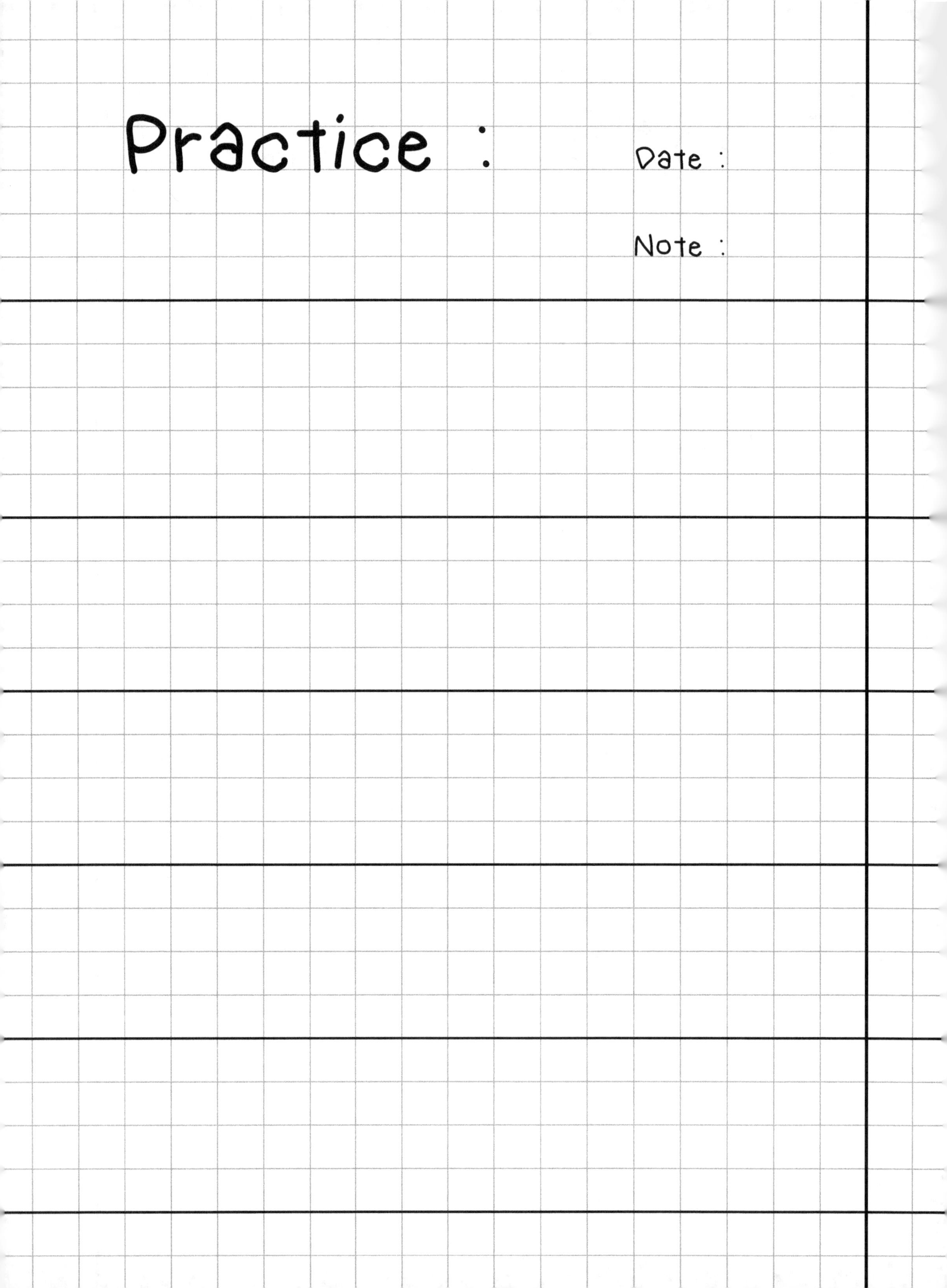

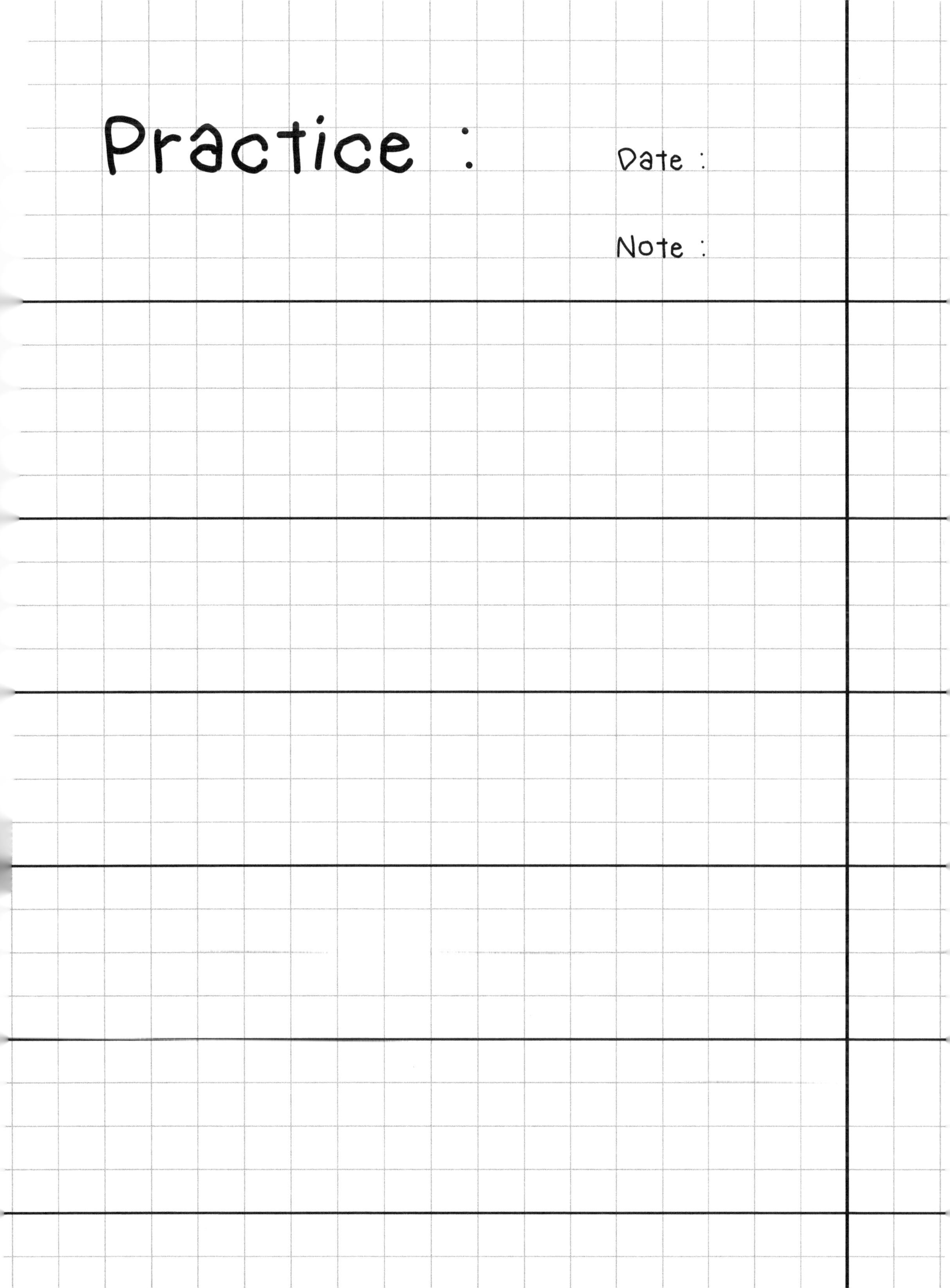

Practice :

Date :

Note :

Practice :

Date :

Note :

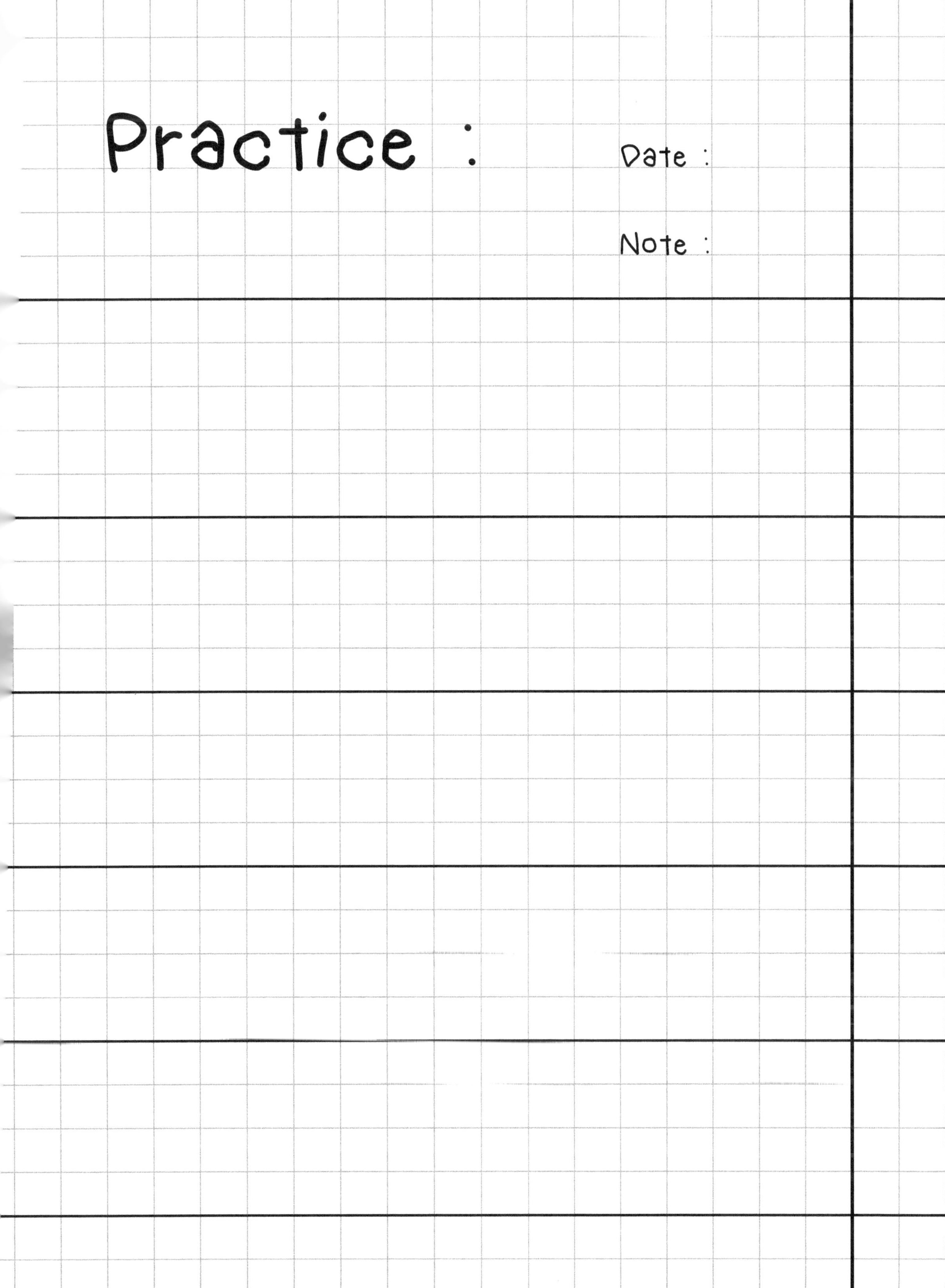

Practice :
Date :
Note :

Practice :

Date :

Note :

Practice :

Date :

Note :

Practice :

Date :

Note :

Practice :
Date :
Note :

Practice :

Date :

Note :

Practice :

Date :

Note :

Practice :

Date :

Note :

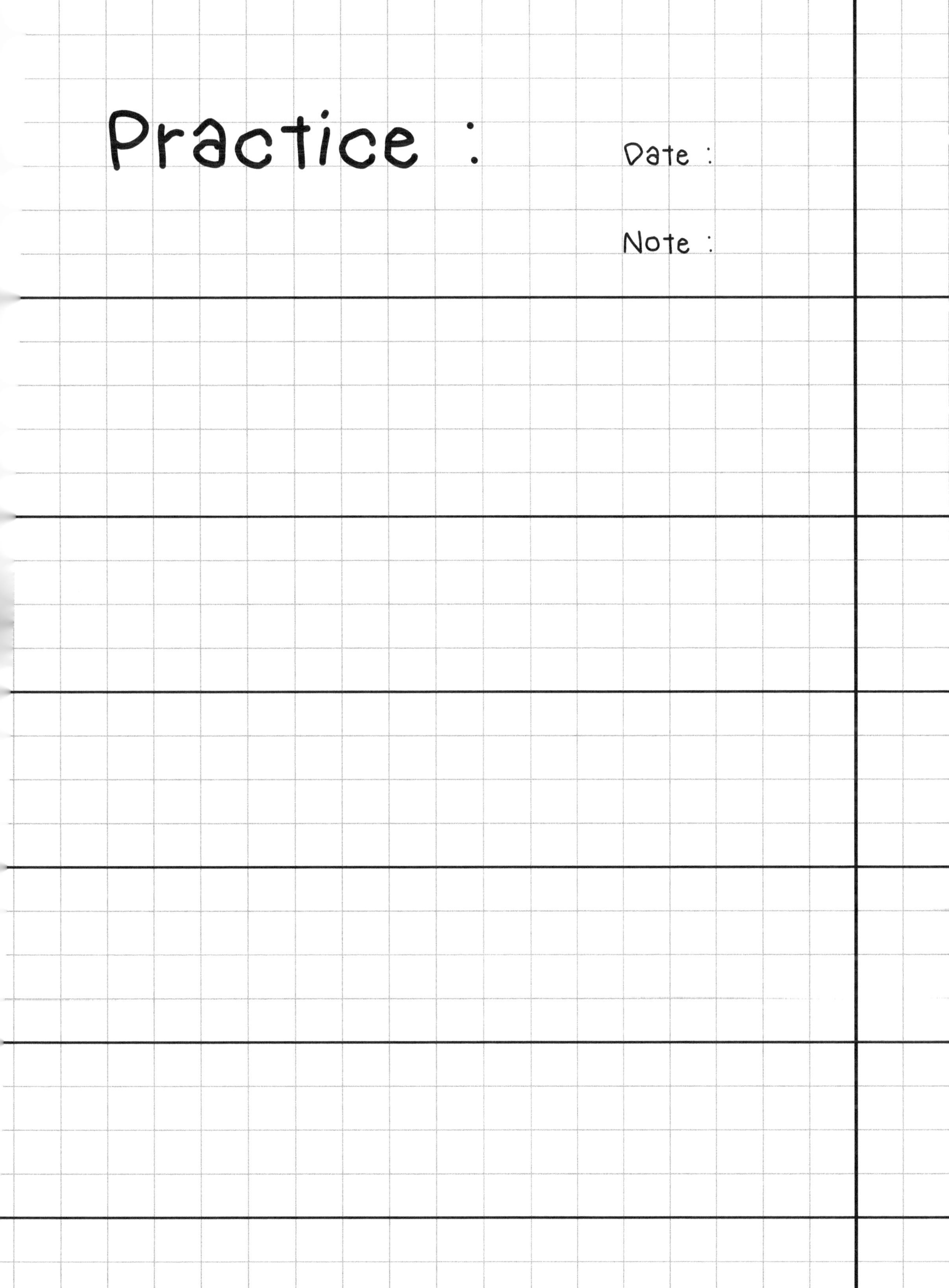
Practice :
Date :
Note :

Practice :

Date :

Note :

Practice :

Date :

Note :

Practice :

Date :

Note :

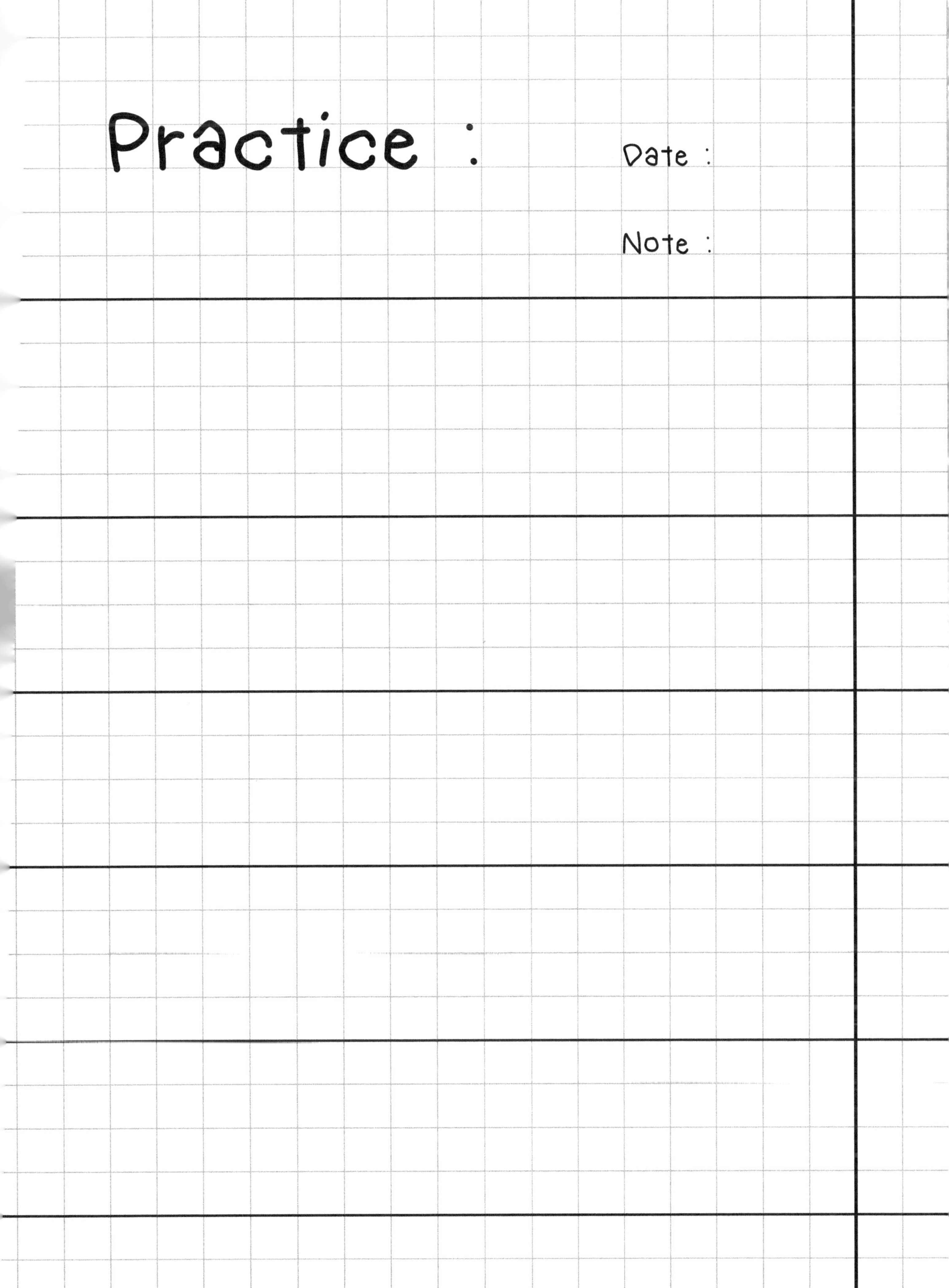
Practice :
Date :
Note :

Practice :

Date :

Note :

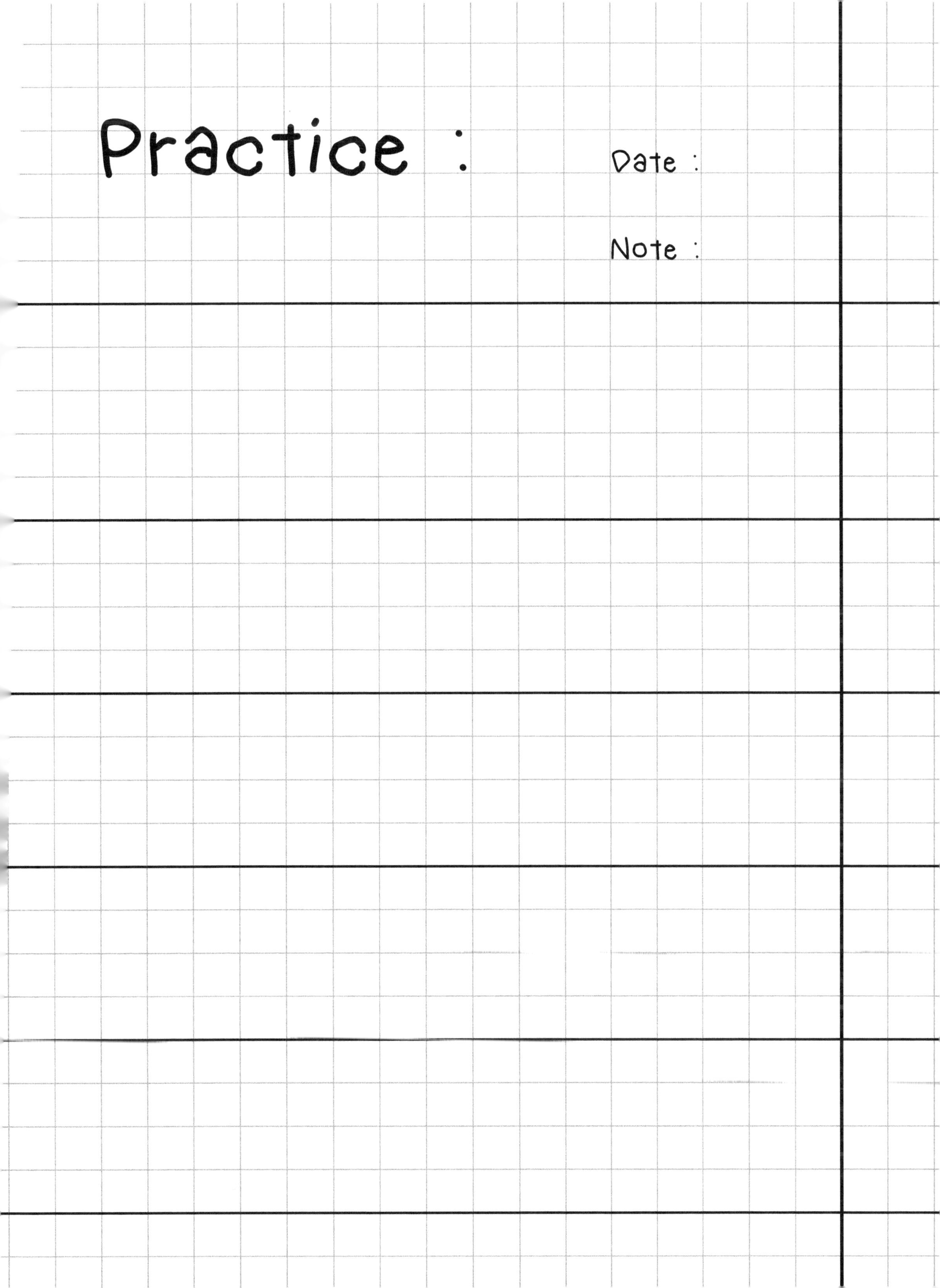

Practice :
Date :
Note :

Practice :

Date :

Note :

Practice :
Date :
Note :

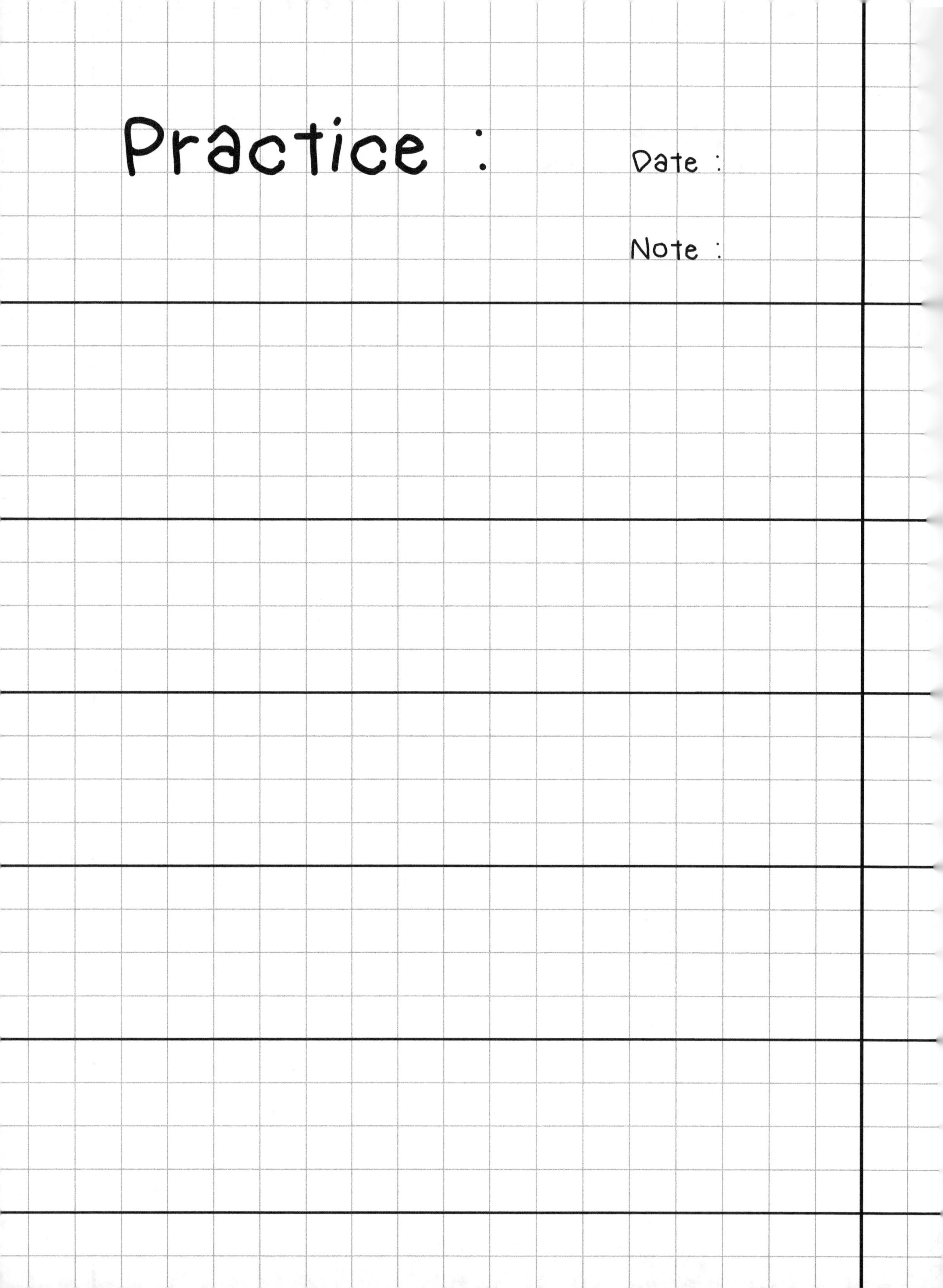
Practice :
Date :
Note :

Practice :

Date :

Note :

Practice :

Date :

Note :

Practice :

Date :

Note :

Practice :

Date :

Note :

Practice :

Date :

Note :

Practice :

Date :

Note :

Practice :

Date :

Note :

Practice :

Date :

Note :

Practice :

Date :

Note :

Practice :   Date :

Note :

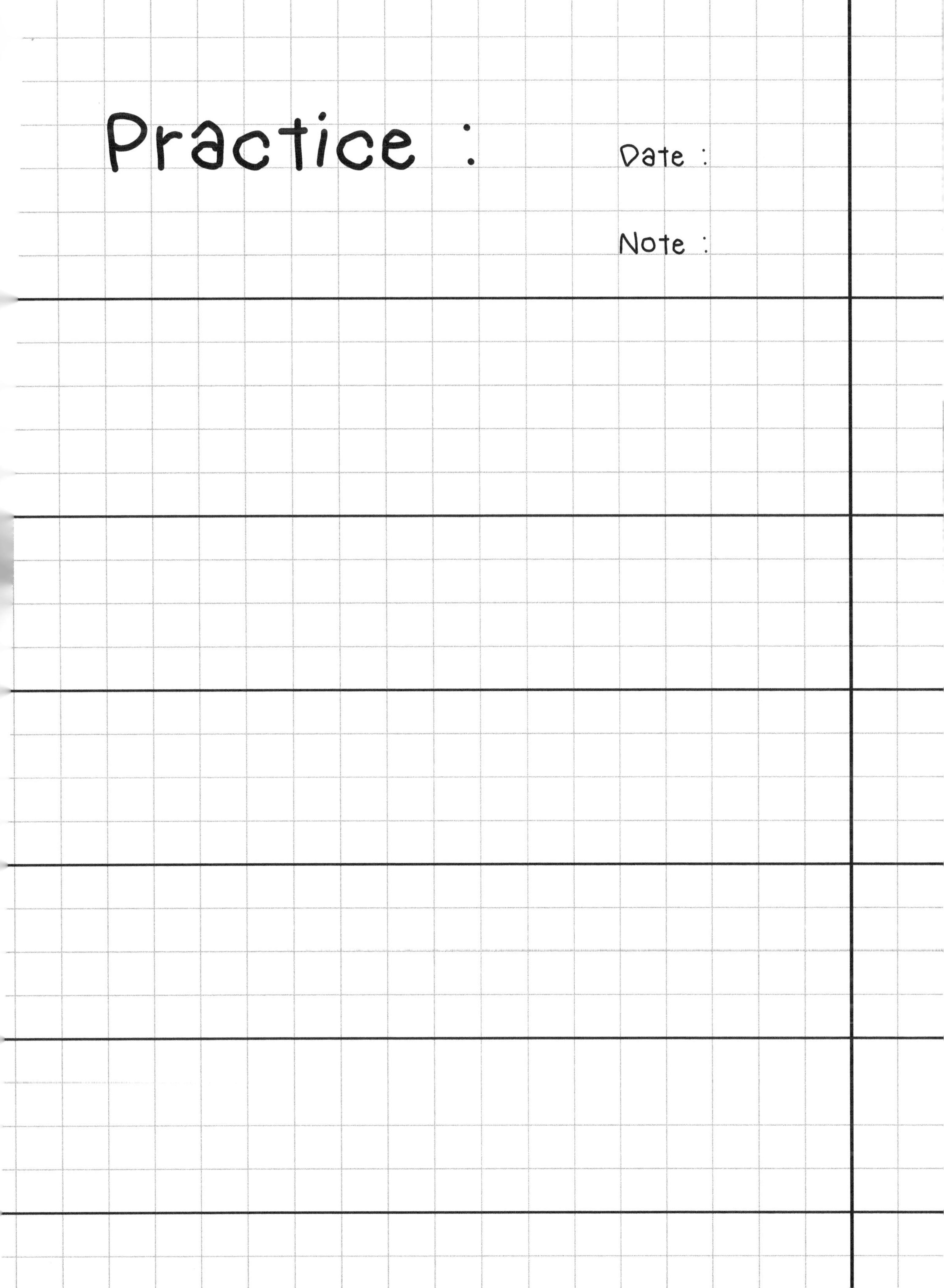

Practice :
Date :
Note :

Practice :

Date :

Note :

www.ingramcontent.com/pod-product-compliance
Lightning Source LLC
Chambersburg PA
CBHW080835160726
47999CB00009B/2903